TROPICAL HOUSES

TROPICAL HOUSES

Imelda Akmal

Equatorial Living Redefined

images Publishing

Published in Australia in 2018 by
The Images Publishing Group Pty Ltd
ABN 89 059 734 431
6 Bastow Place, Mulgrave, Victoria 3170, Australia
Tel: +61 3 9561 5544 Fax: +61 3 9561 4860
books@imagespublishing.com
www.imagespublishing.com

The Images Publishing Group Reference Number: 1282

NATIONAL LIBRARY OF AUSTRALIA

A catalogue record for this book is available from the National Library of Australia

Title: Tropical Houses / Imelda Akmal Architectural Writer Studio (IAAW Studio) (Ed.)
ISBN: 9781864706840 (hardback)

Text and research by IAAW Studio:
Imelda Akmal (Principal), Alicchys Siregar, Dini Kusumawardhani, Ranti Ekaputri, Dinda Mundakir, Diah Puspita Sari, Kanya Pratita Wanaditya, Daniel Jiang, Anggita Triastari
Photography: Sonny Sandjaya Photography, except for the following pages:
Fernando Gomulya, 8–9, 38–43, 140–5; Mario Wibowo, 32–7, 218–223; Sjahrial Iqbal, 92–103, 130 top, 131 bottom, 132, 170–5, 181, 213 top, 215 right, 216 top right and bottom, 224-229; Ivan Priatman, 206-211.
Digital imaging: M. Aluwi
English translation: Jessy Faiz, Dinda Mundakir

Production manager | Group art director: Nicole Boehringer
Senior editor: Gina Tsarouhas
Assisting editor: Hannah Jenkins
Graphic designer: Ryan Marshall

Printed on 140gsm GoldEast Matt Art paper by Toppan Leefung Printing (Shenzhen) Co., Ltd

IMAGES has included on its website a page for special notices in relation to this and its other publications. Please visit www.imagespublishing.com

Contents

Introduction

by Imelda Akmal

The tropics is a term designated for an area located exactly along the Equator, an imaginary line along the sun's path. Geographically, the tropics lies in an area between the northern hemisphere at 23° 26'13.3", or 23.43702° north in the Tropic of Cancer and the southern hemisphere at 23°26'13.3, or 23.43702° south in the Tropic of Capricorn.

The climatic characteristics of the tropics are very unique. The sun rises and sets around the same time, which is quite different from countries with four seasons. Any variation between sunrise and sunset times consists of minutes only.

The characteristics of air temperature are similar to the rising and setting of the sun. In tropical climates, the air temperature rises and falls with a relatively constant difference. The air temperature ranges between 81°F (27°C) and 86°F (30°C)—in some areas it may reach 91°F (33°C)—while the night temperature ranges between 77°F (25°C) and 81°F (27°C). This minor difference creates a comfortable air temperature for the human body. The air temperature in tropical climates only becomes uncomfortable if the temperature exceeds 81°F (27°C). Even then, this discomfort is easily handled by using several methods such as a building design that follows the sun's path, the planting of vegetation to deter extreme weather, and ensuring good air flow and cross ventilation. It is for these reasons that life in the tropics is highly comfortable as well as secure.

The subject of air temperature is so indicative of the tropics that *Bauhaus Magazine* in their June 2013 edition published a commentary specifically about the tropical climate and architecture. In their earlier chapters, Torstein Blume put forward writings about the relationship between tropics and nudity. They explore the idea that due to the warmth of air in the areas of Africa, Asia, and South America, people are comfortable and even freely accepted without clothes. In fact, in certain areas of the tropics many primitive communities are still practicing a nude lifestyle. In Indonesia, people living in remote Papua areas are comfortable going about in their daily life in minimal clothing. Newborn babies are carried in the nude and are free to play in the nude all day. It is similar with the Dayak tribe. Until the 1970s, women on the island of Bali also went about daily life with exposed torsos, wearing cloths only from the waist below. As a result of this nude custom, many Balinese women were the targets of European photographers. In the peaceful villages of Jawa, men and women still go about shirtless, especially the elderly who convey a lifestyle from earlier times.

As such the tropics are often imagined and connected to matters that are exotic, even sensual. Nudity does not only have an impact toward the experience of comfort in a tropical climate, it also conveys a sense of transparency— when we are uncovered we are openly seen. This philosophy also translates into tropical architecture, as it is more open and free-flowing than architecture in four-season countries.

The contrast between tropical-climate architecture and the architecture in four-season countries is undeniable. Those who live with four seasons tend only to be able to experience nudity within their home; those living in the tropics can experience nudity under the sky, sun, and moon. All that is required is a roof for protection from rain. Airflow is also an important consideration as it reduces heat waves. As a result of these factors, many homes within tropical climates are half or completely open. Many designs also incorporate perforated or hollowed-out walls.

Because the whole of Indonesia has a tropical climate, the vernacular architecture manifests in various forms. If we were to look at it in detail, all traditional architecture has been designed to anticipate the obstacles that come with this type of climate. For example, vernaculars of houses in Sunda include a large veranda space at the front of the house, roofed by a wide and open wall-less overhang. This is a space in which intensive daily activities take place. The architecture of the traditional Dayak Sintang tribe mirrors this design. The homes have long verandas enclosed by perforated bamboo walls. These verandas are attached to one another to create a singular building. This design is known as the Kalimantan or Dayak Longhouse.

Balinese homes, however, are the opposite. The Kalimantan Longhouse is a building made up of many units of houses, whereas one Balinese unit is made up of many separate buildings. A different fence segregates each building. The activities of Balinese people are conducted mainly in the outdoor spaces between the buildings. Each building is referred to as a *bale*. A ***bale*** is a small building with a staged or raised floor, which stands without walls and has poles supporting the roof. No walls create free airflow within the *bale*, making it an ideal place for various activities. Houses in Nusa Tenggara and Timor have solid walls and are shaped like cones. This shifts the perspective that houses in the tropics need always be porous and open. The enclosed shape aligns with a culture that involves a lot of outdoor activity beyond the home. This is similar to the traditional communities of Papua, whose lives mostly revolve around outdoor activities beyond the building.

At the center of the discussion surrounding the architectural variations beneath the umbrella of traditional Indonesian housing is the influence of Dutch colonization on the history of Indonesian architecture. This focus is arguably a result of the proficiency of the Dutch to keep detailed documentation of their work in Indonesia during the 19th century. Work was documented by means of photography. The architect's name and the promoter of the building were also recorded. They also kept records of the building material specifications, whether it was local or imported, as well as other important data, such as the date of construction and other processes.

Despite the rich oral culture behind Indonesian architecture by Indonesian people, the meticulous documentation maintained by the Dutch community has made it very easy for any historian or researcher to dissect the history of tropical architecture in Indonesia from a limited perspective.

Indonesian culture, both past and present, is still strongly driven by oral accounts. Within communities, history is delivered from generation to generation through stories, songs, and dances, which can easily disappear or become lost if they are not repeated or performed by future generations. This difference in narrative delivery between the two cultures is consistently attributed as the main reason why Indonesian architecture is often regarded as being dominated by the Dutch narrative. It is indeed true, however, that Dutch settlers endeavored to learn how to build their Indonesian homeland's adaptable style of architecture. Authentic Indonesian tropical dwellings are a result of hundreds of years of knowledge, which has been modified and experimented with as it has been passed down through the generations.

Left: Ben House GP

"...sunlight and cross-ventilation was crucial in creating healthier living environments."

It is no wonder then that the earlier history of the Dutch developing their buildings in Indonesia, using methods that were successful in their homeland, initially resulted in a series of failures. The mistakes evident in the design files include accounts of buildings being constructed too thick or having walls that were too heavy. These early walls were also constructed without eaves to protect them. Without protection, the walls easily spoil as a result of harsh tropical sun and rain. The windowsills and jambs, which are made of timber, also damaged easily. These windows were small and slim, with little or no ventilation slats. Apart from the harsh tropical sun and strong torrential rain, the timber frames of the doors and windows were also easily damaged by insect infestation.

The European model of building in tropical climates is also problematic when it comes to human health. Houses with thick, solid walls and minimal openings result in a dark and unpleasant environment. The scarcity of openings significantly hampers airflow, trapping heat and intensifying humidity. These dark and stale spaces promote bacteria growth and foster diseases that can easily transmit to people in this environment, especially tuberculosis because the bacteria thrive in dark spaces. Disease-carrying pests or rodents, such as rats, which thrive in culverts and dark spaces, or mosquitos vectoring malaria and dengue, are an ever-present threat. Therefore, dark spaces that are stuffy and warm are the main problems in Dutch buildings developed in Indonesia during the early years of colonization.

The Dutch administration in Indonesia began to think seriously about resolving such unhealthy dwelling issues after a disease outbreak that caused the death of many Dutch troops in Indonesia. They began to realize a critical mistake: the air in tropical climates is not something that should be contained or blocked in a massive, solid, and enclosed building, on the contrary, sunlight and cross-ventilation was crucial in creating healthier living environments.

Opposite: Pramestha Residence
Following pages: AM House

"...technologies and material developments have allowed architects to explore beyond boundaries and adapt Western modernist design to tropical architecture."

They learned from traditional Indonesian architecture that airflow must be able to move freely and penetrate buildings. As a result, the Dutch began to adapt their designs to include tropical features. The architecture began to evolve with open verandas at the front and rear of the houses and lengthy cantilevered roofs to protect the buildings from rain intrusion. They also began designing large picture windows to allow passages of sunlight and airflow. The architectural style of the Dutch then changed again when the Dutch troops in Indonesia were allowed to bring their wives into the country. The wives of the Dutch administration had a significant impact on architectural design, especially when it came to the home. These women recruited architects, as well as building craftsmen, and instructed them to build homes that aligned with their tastes, taking into consideration the context of the tropical land on which they would be built. Dutch architecture in Indonesia reached its peak when several Dutch architects were given the opportunity to design buildings in Indonesia, particularly in Java. Henri Maclaine Pont, Thomas Karsten, C. P. W. Schoemaker, and P. A. J. Moojen are four of the most productive Dutch architects and they greatly influenced the development of tropical architecture in Indonesia at that time. Their influence would be further enhanced by their admission for tenure in the 1920s, especially Maclaine Pont and Schoemaker, who taught architecture at the Technical Institute of Bandung, which was then called Technische Hoogeschool. Their influence is still recognized today.

When considering architecture within tropical climates today, it is important to acknowledge the variety of design approaches available and how these enable architects to respond to the challenges of nature. Another important factor to consider is the development of technology. These days there are many new technologies available to tackle obstacles that may cause discomfort in the tropical climate. The most significant technology that has modified the pattern of designing and planning in tropical climates is the discovery of air conditioning and air-handling units. It is not an ideal solution for many reasons, including the impact on the environment, but it has grown to be the most widespread and easiest way of cooling down any space. Other technologies involving digital sensors further ease the architect's responsibility. These sensors vary the angle of sun-shading fins, which protect a building from direct sunlight. The final factor is the development of building materials. Currently, waterproofing materials, such as high-quality concrete, are widely available in markets. With this type of concrete, many tropical houses no longer require large overhangs but can instead have flat concrete roofs. These styles of roofs are commonly topped with grass or pools, which reduces heat gain inside the building. Also widely available are glass materials with heat-absorbing layers as well as ultraviolet protection, which assist when a building requires large window areas. Other materials like thermal-proof and weatherproof paint have also enabled architects to be more flexible in their design.

These technologies and material developments have allowed architects to explore beyond boundaries and adapt Western modernist design to tropical architecture. This has had a significant impact on the variety and type of design approaches taken by architects designing homes within tropical climates. It is important to keep a critical mind regarding the impact of the designs illustrated in this book, environmental, societal, or otherwise. Has the design approach given positive contribution to the surrounding society, environment, and context? Are new ideas being contributed or innovative solutions offered? Ask yourself these questions as you become immersed in the beautiful content. Happy reading and we hope that you find this book a source of inspiration.

A House

Tangerang Selatan, South Jakarta
Budi Pradono Architects

Resident comfort is the main focus in the design of A House. The architect wanted to create a home in which his client, who works in a highly demanding profession as an orthopaedic surgeon, could experience optimal relaxtion. Located in Tangerang Selatan, the site remains occupied by extensive areas of greenery. The architect took advantage of these surrounds and presented a building based on a concept of transparency, allowing the resident to enjoy nature from inside the house.

The avoidance of a Madagascar almond tree, which existed on the site, determined the building's form. The tree was a gift from the owner's friend and planted on the site ten years ago. The architect resolved to keep it due to client's interest in collecting rare trees. Based on this fact, the architect also proposed to plant more trees on the site and even inside the building.

The house consists of three stories, with the second and third levels supported by exposed-steel structures. The use of exposed steel is an architectural expression intended to represent the spirit and character of the client. The concept of transparency is referenced once again through the application of clear glass on the façade. The lush green trees and raised soil at the ground level solve issues of privacy associated with the home's transparency.

Left: The top floor functions as a resting area with the master bedroom, bathroom, and powder room.

Each story of the building was built with a different function. The ground floor was designed as a kitchen and dining area, the second floor as the living area, and the third floor as the master bedroom. A continuous wooden staircase connects all floors. These pared-down functions are intended to create an intimate atmosphere for the client. According to the architect, "humans will increasingly detach themselves from things that they do not need. A dwelling designed for those who have reached personal maturity should return to the basics of living, dining, and resting."

Inside the home, a milkwood pine tree surrounded by glass is visible from each floor. The third-floor bathroom, separated from the master bedroom by glass, also enjoys a view of the tree. The bathroom was designed as a wide space and is intended to balance the client's busy life. It is a space in which the occupants can refresh and prepare for the next day's activities.

Top left: The spacious bathroom has been designed as the owner's private relaxation space. **Top right:** Each floor is connected by one continuous wooden staircase. **Bottom right:** From the bedroom, the glass façade provides a framed view of the lush greenery.

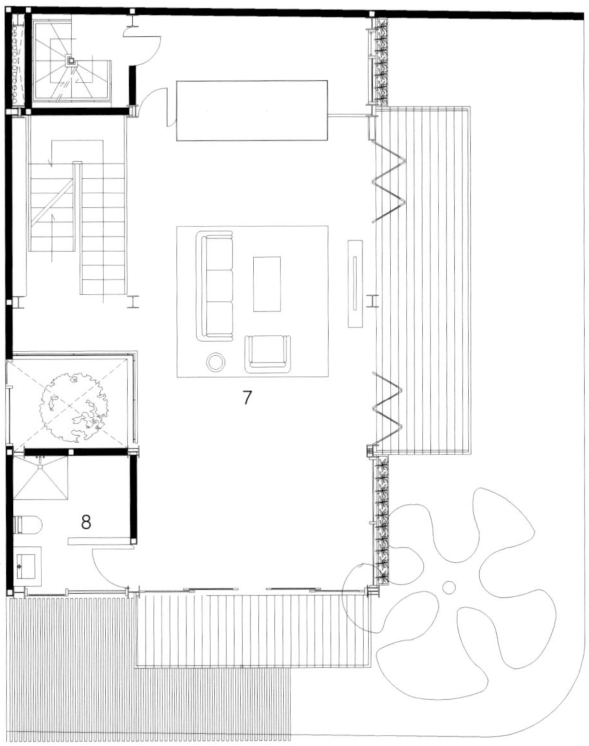

First-floor plan

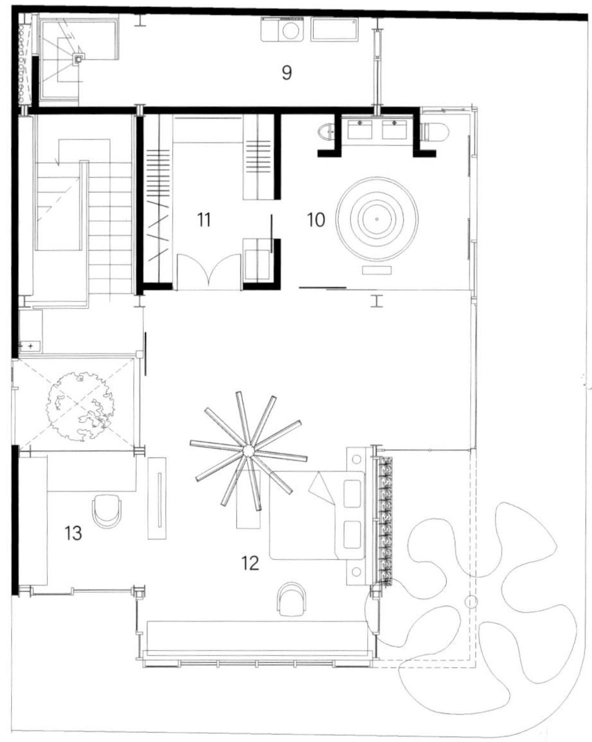

Second-floor plan

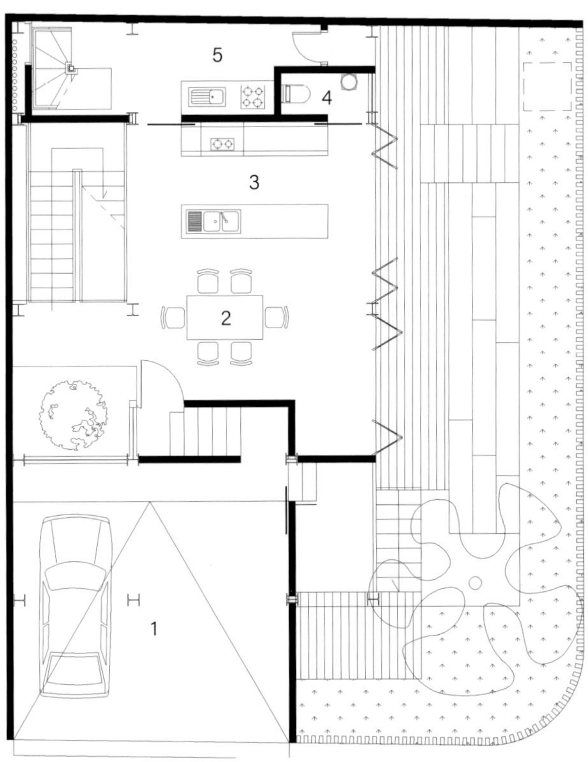

Ground-floor plan

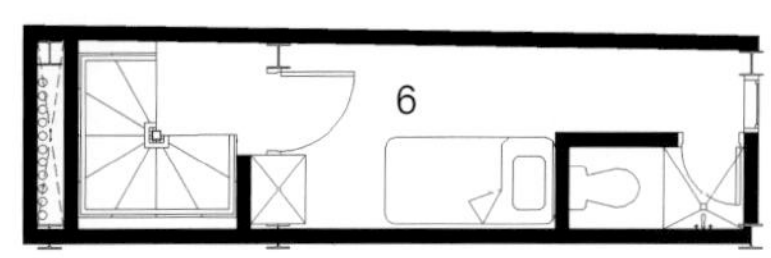

Mezzanine floor plan

1 Carport
2 Dining room
3 Pantry
4 Powder room
5 Kitchen
6 Maid's room
7 Living room
8 Bathroom
9 Washing and drying area
10 Master bathroom
11 Wardrobe
12 Master bedroom
13 Study room

0 2m

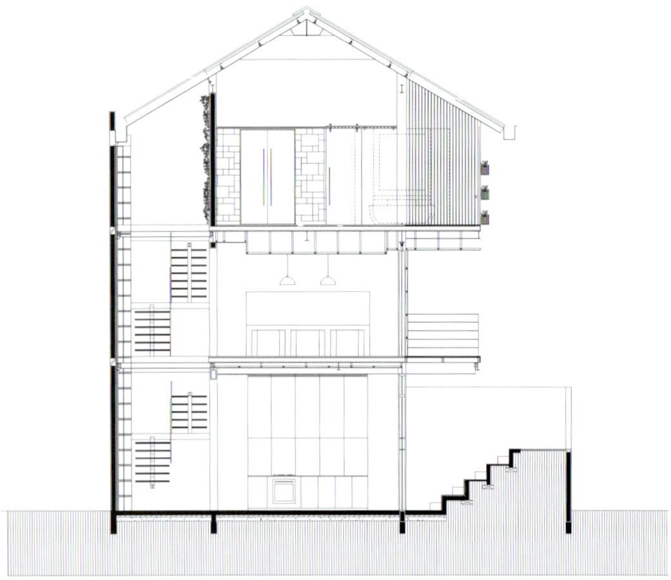

Section one

Using glass as a primary material posed potential problems of noise pollution from the road and heat from direct sunlight. The site is located at an intersection of residential streets, which results in high traffic during rush hours. In order to solve these issues, the architect created a sound barrier from elevated soil at the ground level, which also doubles as an amphitheatre. On the façade, double glass is used to reduce noise and solar heat. In this instance, avoiding heat did not also mean avoiding sunlight from entering the house.

To preserve the Madagascar almond tree on site, the building was designed on the corner beside the neighbor's wall. This placement resulted in limited access to sunlight for many parts of the building. To manage this, the architect applied laser-cut perforated ceilings from stainless material to allow light inside the building, while also giving the home a wide impression.

In addition to its modern identity, A House also incorporates an internal experience of nature. Steel and glass used in combination with wooden floors and stone walls create an ambience in complete opposition to the client's workplace. Successfully translating the client's needs into optimal living spaces was of the utmost importance to the architect.

Left: A deck located on the middle floor functions as a space to sit back and enjoy the refreshing view. **Middle and right:** The area around the Madagascar almond tree has been utilized as both garden and gathering space that descends below the ground. **Opposite:** From the road at the front, the building appears concealed by lush trees.

Site Area: 1970 ft² (183 m²) **Total Floor Area:** 3444 ft² (320 m²) **Photographer:** Sonny Sandjaya **Design Period:** 2009 **Construction Period:** 2010–2013 **Design Principal:** Budi Pradono **Assistant Architect:** Hendrawan Setyanegara, Ayu Diah Shanty, Jimmyongo, Anton Suryono **Studio Support:** Desti Amelia, David Aryanto Poeyamidjaya, Tutto Ardito, Zuardin Akbar, Atika Nur F. **Model Maker:** Daryanto, Atika Nur Fitriana **Interior:** Budi Pradono Architects **Landscape:** Budi Pradono Architects **Contractor:** Mega Sarana, Sukari **Structure:** PT Toyo Cahya Engineering **M&E:** Mega Sarana, Sukari **Lighting:** Budi Pradono Architects

AA House

Pantai Indah Kapuk, Jakarta
Nataneka Arsitek

Contemporary urban homes are often sleek in appearance and designed with clean-cut angles. Following this trend toward minimalist chic, many stylish city homes take shape as an arrangement of geometric forms. Instead of relying on decorative ornaments, these homes flaunt fascinating compositions, finished with luxurious materials. The design expression of AA House, located in one of Jakarta's prime residential areas, can be considered an example of this approach.

The home's façade appears as a composition of cuboid volumes. Solid boxes are stacked upon one another, subtly interlocking with varying lengths of protrusion. The massing's seemingly additive logic is balanced with the subtracted appearance of deep-set window openings. The depth of these openings provides shade against bright sunlight. Overhanging volumes are either supported by a jutting wall layered in natural stone or intersected with contrasting wooden frames on the upper floors. The volumetric interplay of the façade creates a sense of mystery about how inside spaces might link to one another.

Left: A connecting terrace shades the rooftop lounge at the entry stairwell, and is framed at the end by a rectangular box.

Built for a client who wanted a dwelling with a variety of functions, AA House's spatial design answers questions of accommodation upon a relatively compact site. In addition to living, dining, and bedroom spaces, the house also contains a home theatre, a study space for children's private lessons, and a working area to support the owner's business from home. Despite the project's extensive programme, the architect avoided a single-mass volume for the building. Instead, it is broken down into arranged groups, which are apparent from the façade. Areas of the home are vertically composed into four levels, as well as horizontally into a variety of solid floors and voids.

Beginning from the ground level, the composition is enclosed as a means of separating the private residence from the public road. This level was designed specifically for the home's theatre and service functions. A carport fills one side of the floor and is bordered at the back by an air well, which extends vertically throughout all the floors. Three air wells bring much-needed natural ventilation to the outwardly enclosed ground floor, helping cool the area amidst hot tropical temperatures.

While the service entrance can be accessed from the ground level, the main entrance is placed overhead on the second level. Outdoor steps lead to a shaded porch on the corner of the site, opening up to a subtly concealed side entrance. This floor houses the semi-public activities of the house, including the multifunction room, which can be used for business and children's private lessons. The majority of floor space houses the family's living and dining area, which is bordered by wooden decks that lead to an open-air swimming pool. Despite being on the second level, the pool gives these spaces a sense of grounding.

On the third level, the building's horizontally interlacing spaces become apparent.

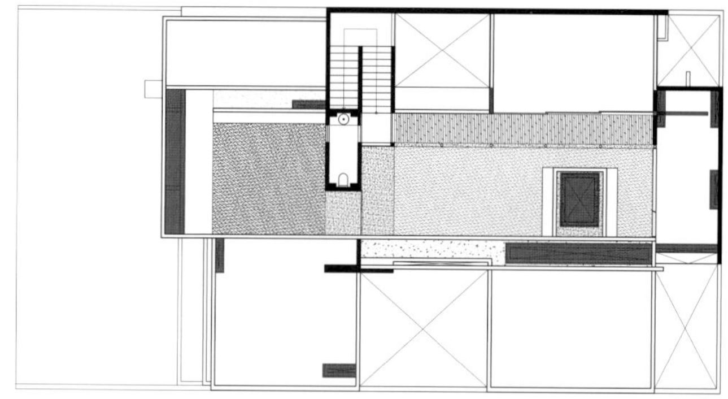

Third-floor plan

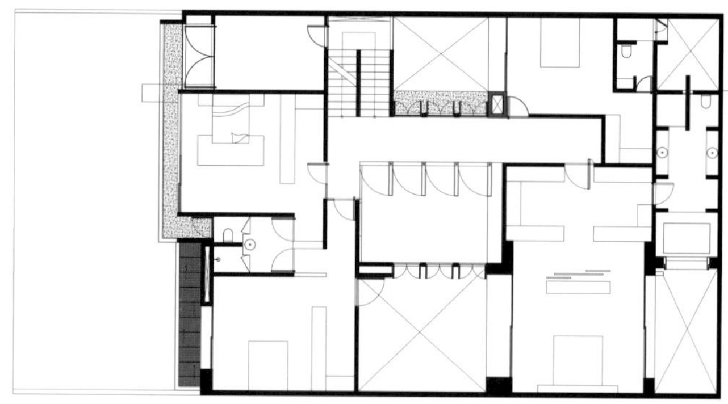

Second-floor plan

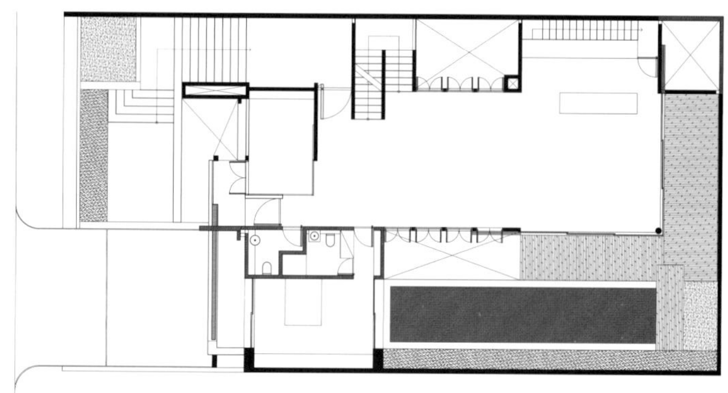

First-floor plan

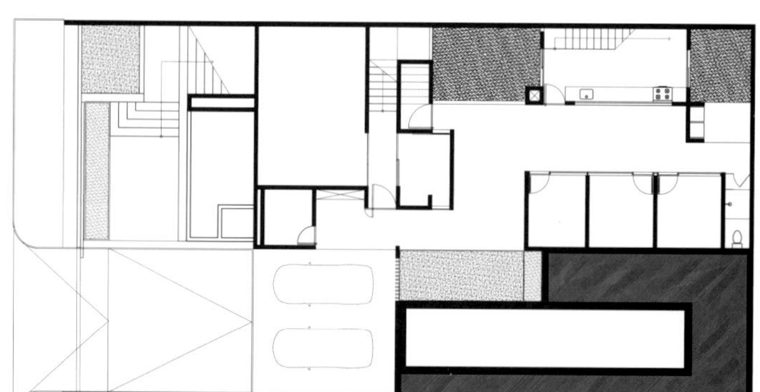

Ground-floor plan

0 4m

Opposite: The façade speaks of volumetric addition and subtraction. Cuboid masses are arranged atop one another and punctuated by the subtracted openings of the windows.

Site Area: 4844 ft² (450 m²) **Floor Area:** 8234 ft² (765 m²) **Photographer:** Martin Westlake **Design Period:** 2009 **Construction Period:** 2010
Design Principal: Jeffry Sandy, Sukendro Sukendar Priyoso **Design Team:** Endy Ersal

AA House

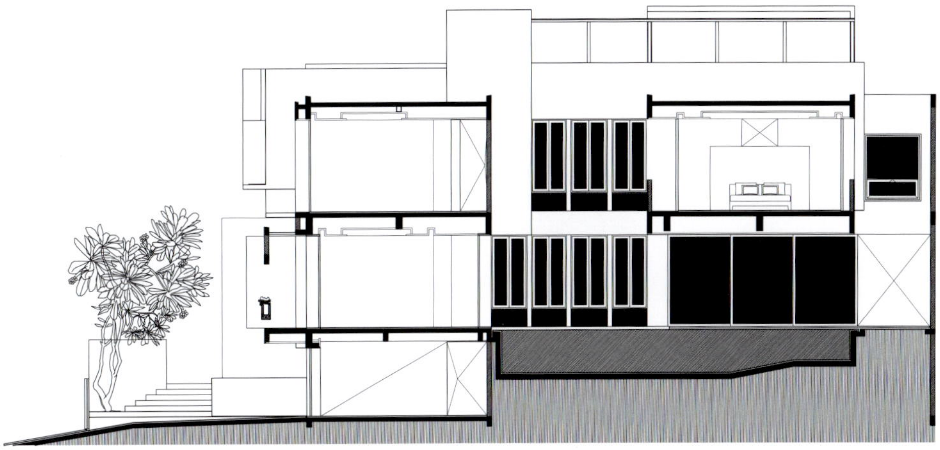

Longitudinal section

The main bedroom hovers across the swimming pool, with windows on either side opening up to air wells. This ensures natural ventilation within the space and gives the room a dramatic, suspended in mid-air feeling. All of the spaces on the third floor, as well as the children's play area, are linked to air wells or outdoor views. Despite the openness, their placement on the third level provides a higher measure of privacy.

The mass becomes even less enclosed at the fourth level. A lounge, sitting amidst a roof garden of ornamental pebbles and green grass, takes advantage of the flat roof. A shaded walkway runs parallel against the lounge, connecting it to a stairwell entrance. Ahead, a rectangular box frames this entrance, while setting it back from the street view. This box provides a thread of continuity and a closure for the cuboid volumes composed throughout the design.

Opposite top left: The doors throughout the house are crafted from engineered teak wood. **Opposite top right:** Natural materials such as wood have been used extensively for the furniture and finishes, balancing the clear-cut geometries of the architecture. **Opposite bottom:** Air wells have been placed in between spaces, such as the corner of the swimming pool deck. **Left:** The main bedroom hovers across the swimming pool, providing shade for swimming even on sunny days.

AM House

Bintaro, South Jakarta

andramatin

The home of Andra Matin, one of Indonesia's most progressive architects whose works are often identified as radically contemporary, was evidently based on the architect's admiration for Indonesia's vernacular architecture. However, unlike most designs, it was not immediately translated through its forms, but rather, through the depth of its essence by way of spatial exploration. As a result, the home is able to retain its contemporary flavors. The design was inspired by traditional stilt houses, which maintain a strong connection with their environment. These stilt houses were also the basis for the design exploration of this home, with its open spaces and minimal solid walls. The home itself is a manifestation of the desire to integrate a spacious garden as part of the home.

The contemporary characteristics of Andra Matin's designs are clearly discernable in the combination of concrete and worn ironwood used as the main materials for this house. Although it may appear unfinished, the design was more focused on the treatment of height differences, calculating width, playing with open areas, and composing light and dark. According to the architect, 'the home offers poetic spatial experiences and accommodates a spatial program not usually found in homes.'

Left: The decision to get rid of walls created a certain spatial luxury, and the garden plays a central role in that respect.

Top: The façade of the house at night. **Bottom:** Exposure to rain is a consequence of incorporating an open design in a tropical region with high precipitation. **Opposite top:** Rough, unfinished concrete alongside worn ironwood. The durability of the concrete and the fact that termites detest ironwood make this design durable and easily maintainable. **Opposite middle:** The master bedroom is separated from the main building, an unavoidable consequence of the architect's wish to bring a large garden inside the house. **Opposite bottom:** The living room is adjacent to the dining room. Both rooms become the main area in this home.

The sound of the breeze as it ripples across the surface of the pool creates a serene atmosphere in the front porch. The semi-open porch is located opposite the architect's private library, which is a room surrounded by glass walls. Dim light emanating from the library illuminates the dark rows of ironwood dominating the spaces on the ground floor. The rest of the ground floor is used to accommodate secondary spaces such as the garage, storage area, and service area.

A wooden ramp leads around to the library and up to the next floor. Here, open spaces and a garden act as the home's center for activities. These spaces were designed to be as open as possible—no walls, doors, or windows. The absence of any kind of separator—except for the structural columns supporting the mass above this area—makes the stilt house inspiration for the design obvious. The living room, dining room, and pantry merge into a single large area. This acts as a communal space where family members can gather. This unique configuration and its elimation of obstructions allows for both visual and physical enjoyment of the garden. On the oppsite side of the garden there is a swimming pool, which further enhances the element of nature within the house.

The desire to present a large garden as a part of the home presented design challenges.

Site Area: 4069 ft² (378 m²) **Floor Area:** 6781 ft² (630 m²) **Photographer:** Sonny Sandjaya **Design Period:** 2007–2010 **Construction Period:** 2008–2010
Design Principal: Andra Matin **Design Team:** Asep Tatang **Landscape:** Andra Matin **Contractor:** Alex Gandung

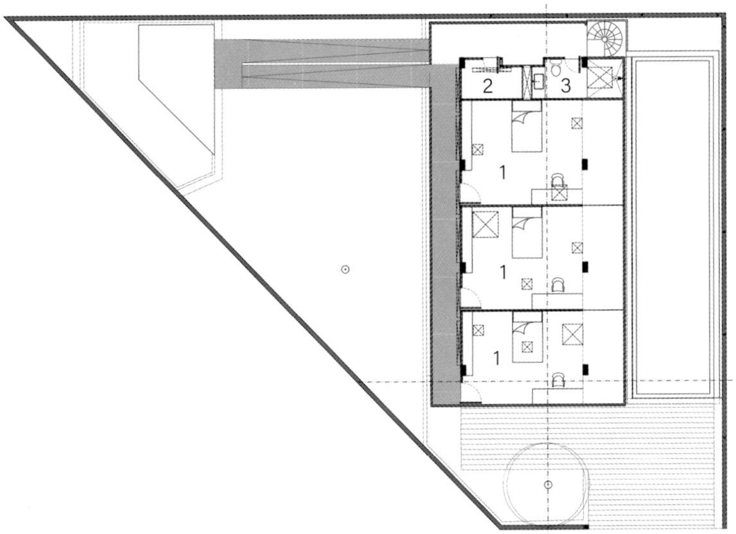

Second-floor plan

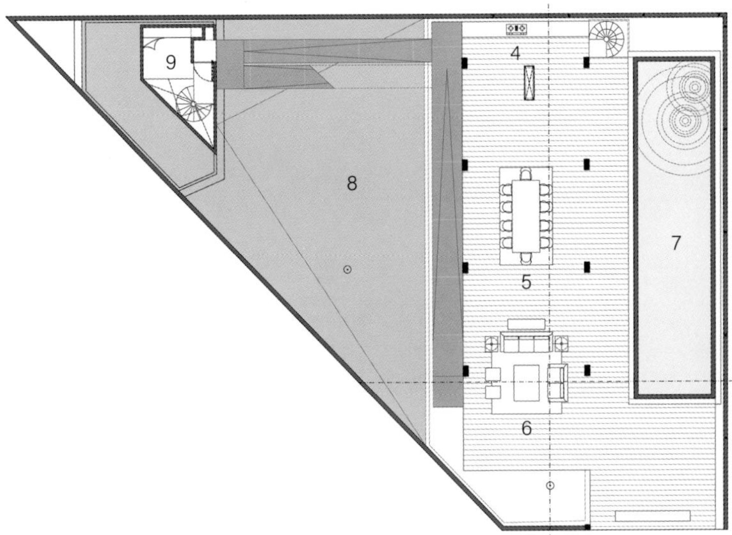

First-floor plan

1 Bedroom
2 Storage
3 Bathroom
4 Pantry
5 Dining room
6 Living room
7 Swimming pool
8 Garden
9 Master bedroom
10 Master bathroom
11 Maid's room
12 Maid's bathroom
13 Powder room
14 *Musholla* (congregational space)
15 Library
16 Garage
17 Ramp
18 Pond

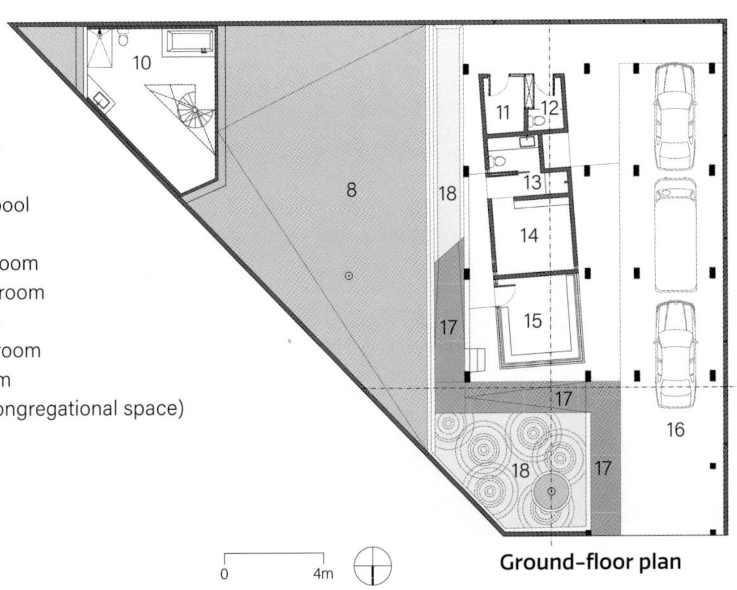

Ground-floor plan

Upon designing the position of the bedroom, the architect realized that a merging of the master bedroom with the main building would reduce the size of the garden and make the bedroom lose its open space. It was decided that the master bedroom would be separated from the main building and designed as a small, asymmetric concrete building, appearing as a sculpture at the end of the garden.

Located on the next floor are the children's bedrooms. This area of the house is accessed via a ramp that crosses above the garden before leading upwards. The ramp was designed as an uncovered walkway without railings, and exposes itself to the natural environment that merges with the house. A circulation route wraps around this enclosed space and permeates a private atmosphere throughout the floor. All three bedrooms have been merged into a single large space. Sleeping areas are hidden behind three white cubes one meter above the surface of the floor. This design generates warm personal spaces. Inspired by capsule hotels found in Japan, the architect was quite bold in his experimentation for the space, especially considering it was created for children. The master bedroom, which has been separated from the main building by a garden, demonstrates the architect's maximum tolerance for nature and the outdoors as well as the various atmospheres achieved throughout the house.

The radical design of this home was not sought through external architectural influences but born out of the personal needs of the architect. Both the concept and design process were unusual. The architect designed the project without any working drawings. Instead, all design was done in situ and relied on direct communication with the builders.

Opposite top left: As a place intended only for sleep, the bedroom is a small and intimate space.
Opposite top right & bottom: The main bathroom is uniquely designed under the bedroom.

Bangka House

South Jakarta
d-associates architect

The Bangka area is located near the entertainment area of Kemang and is known for its bustling streets and heavy traffic. In response to the context and potential security and privacy issues, d-associates designed the house with a solid façade to protect the occupants. The bare concrete used for the façade signifies a sense of unity between the house and the modern urban area. The terrace and the front yard have been designed to transition from the busy streets to inside areas of the house.

In contrast to the surrounding urban area, the clients want to incorporate nature as part of the house. The architect interpreted the clients' demands by injecting a Zen concept into the design. In an effort to create a balance between nature and the urban landscape, a natural barrier was offered as a solution.

A perimeter wall filled with plants surrounds the house. The plants produce fresh air, minimize heat, and improve the microclimate inside the house. Furthermore, the plants filter noise from the street, while creating a peaceful ambience.

Left: The home's distinctive mass is suspended alongside the pool, echoing its geometry.

Top & opposite top: By retracting the glass sliding doors, the house achieves a spacious living area by blending the indoor with the outdoor. **Bottom left:** The indoor and outdoor areas are separated by glass partitions. **Bottom right:** From the outside, the house seems to be closed off with minimum openings.

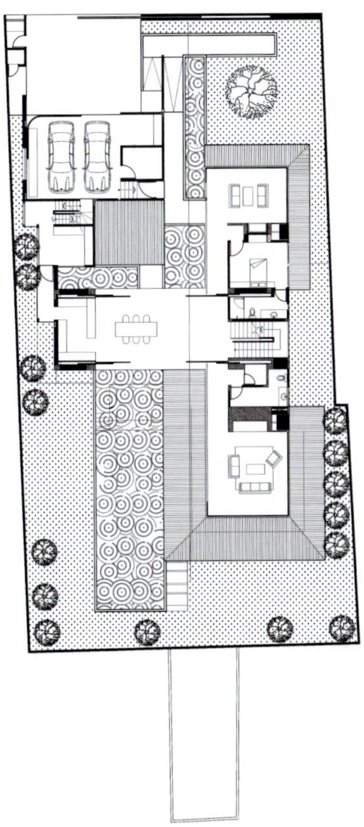

Ground-floor plan

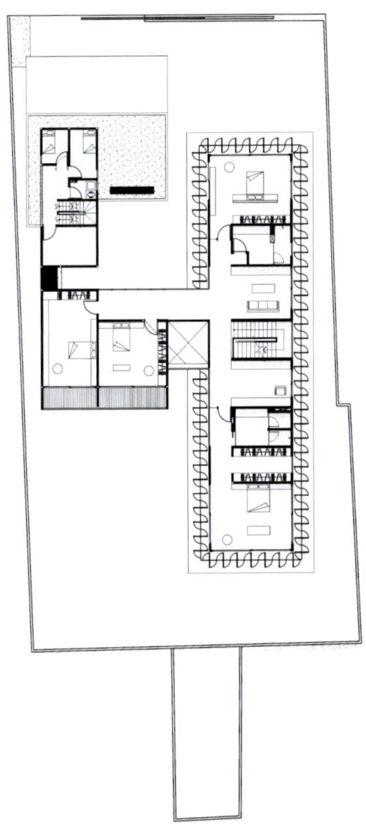

Upper-floor plan

Instead of facing the main street, the house orients toward the backyard and swimming pool. The L-shaped configuration of the building mass encloses the swimming pool. To ensure all rooms within the house receive the same amount of air and light, each mass is elongated. To allow for the interaction of space on the ground floor, the use of solid outer walls has been avoided. Instead, small wooden partitions define boundaries. This achieves an inclusion of the outdoor atmosphere and creates continuity between human interaction and air circulation.

The idea of openness has been applied to the design of the ground floor. It is a communal space that also accommodates guests. A 30-foot-long (9-meter-long) cantilever from the upper floor shelters the living room and fulfills the desire for an open space by eliminating the need for columns. This design solution allows occupants to move freely around the terrace, swimming pool, and dining room. Movable glass partitions have been installed around the ground floor for privacy.

In contrast to the communal focus of the ground floor, the upper floor is a private space. Located at the end of the cantilever is the master bedroom, which is flanked by other bedrooms. To allow for sunlight and air to move freely into the bedrooms, the sides that orient toward the swimming pool have been designed with glass boundaries. The architect decided to increase the privacy level of the master bedroom by enclosing the upper mass with black woven shades. These shades create a sunscreen for the master bedroom and are a striking accent to the gray and white walls. They can also be rotated to create varied spatial experiences caused by the movement of shadows and light during the day. Installed at a certain distance, the sunscreen creates a walkway around the upper floor, granting access to other rooms.

In conjunction with the program and room configuration, the architect also uses aesthetic elements to support a calming atmosphere throughout the house. Dark floor tiles, wooden partitions, and wooden furniture all induce this atmosphere. Several small ponds located in different corners of the house allow occupants to feel refreshed by the sound of trickling water. Together with the greenery surrounding the house, these details succeed in creating an ambient and serene escape from the chaotic city.

Top: Operable black-woven screens enclose the distinctive mass. **Middle:** The bedroom exudes a warm atmosphere with parquet and wooden furniture. The woven enclosure protects the room from glaring sunlight. **Bottom:** The woven screens project a unique pattern of sunshade on the wall, which moves with the sun's position. **Opposite:** Designed to be more spacious than the lower level, a cantilever formed by the upper floor's mass shelters the front terrace.

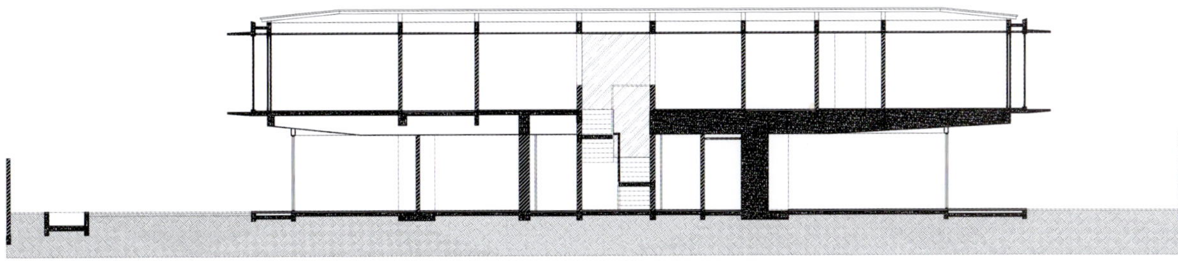

Longitudinal section

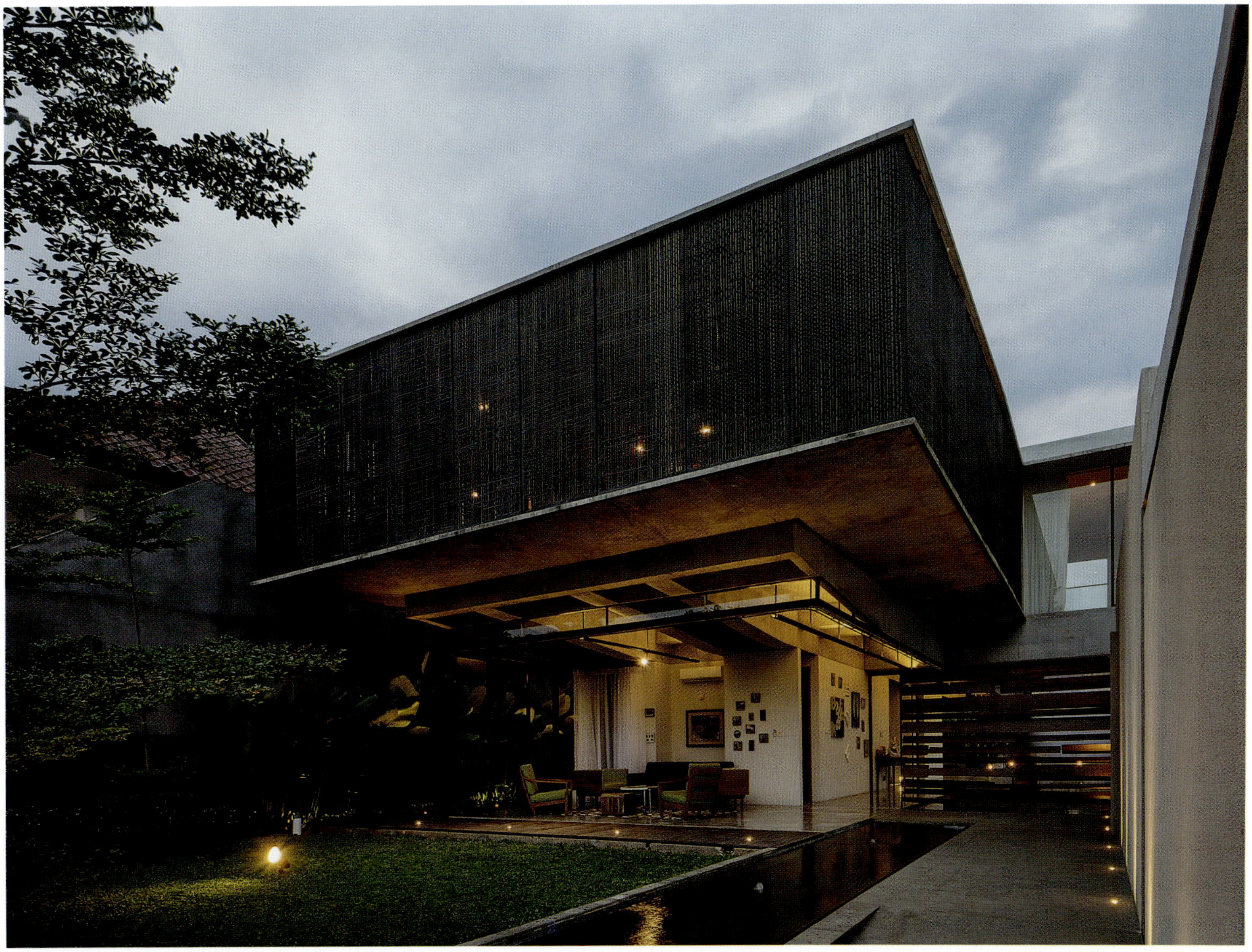

Site Area: 11,840 ft² (1100 m²) **Floor Area:** 8611 ft² (800 m²) **Photographer:** Mario Wibowo **Design Period:** 2009–2010 **Construction Period:** 2010–2011 **Design Principal:** Gregorius Supie Yolodi, Maria Rosantina **Design Team:** Sony Restu Wibowo, Yukti Atyanta **Interior:** d-associates architect and owner **Contractor:** Syarif **Structure:** Muchammad Umar **M&E:** Rusman Riadi **Lighting:** Lenny, Lentera Lighting

Ben House GP

South Jakarta

GeTs Architects

Situated on a 4306-square-foot (400-square-meter) site, the client wanted a big and modern home with generous space to accommodate his activities. His love of natural elements posed a challenge for the architect: how to create a large and spacious home with a swimming pool without sacrificing open space.

Based on these requests, the architect offered a compact design solution. One of the space-saving ideas was to orient the conventional open-space garden vertically.

The vertical garden floods the house with fresh air without taking up too much space. Placed on the wall beside the swimming pool, the garden gives natural nuance to the home.

A strong emphasis on the natural environment is also demonstrated in the openness between the outdoor area and interior. The building mass is designed to enfold the swimming pool in a U-shaped configuration, exposing the space to the swimming pool and vertical garden. In contrast to the relatively enclosed façade, the boundaries between the interior space and swimming pool are made of glass, offering a unified feeling between indoors and outdoors. This blurring of space gives the living room an outdoor terrace feel. The large amount of sunshine that enters the upper story is filtered by vertical wooden slats, which also act as a decorative element.

Left: Owing to the building's U-shaped mass, the occupants can enjoy a pool, garden, and open-air courtyard.

Creating a more enclosed look, the slats indicate private spaces. This is a result of the architect deliberately dividing each story based on its level of privacy. The basement functions as a service area with its own circulation, while the first floor is used as a semi-private area. The second floor functions as a private area for the family, with the parents' workspace and children's study space the only communal areas on the floor. These two functions have been merged to support the family's interaction. The semi-private floor connects to the second floor via slim, freestanding stairs. Gaps added at the side of the stairs keep them separate from the wall and create a lightweight feeling. The stairs are located at the opposite side of the swimming pool. This is the darker corner of the house, an area that does not receive enough sunlight. To solve this issue, aluminum bars topped with glass material serve as a wall and roof, and become a light well through which the sun can shine.

Top left: The refreshing view of the greenery becomes an interesting complement to the spacious bedroom. **Middle left:** Living and working spaces are refreshed with views of the vertical garden. **Right:** The architect's idea of unifying the built space with natural space is well executed with extensive openings. A set of metal bars installed in front of the openings block rainwater from splashing inside.

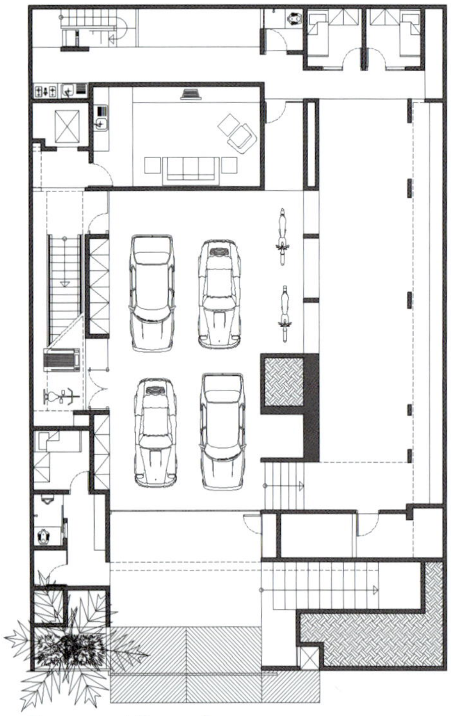

Basement floor plan

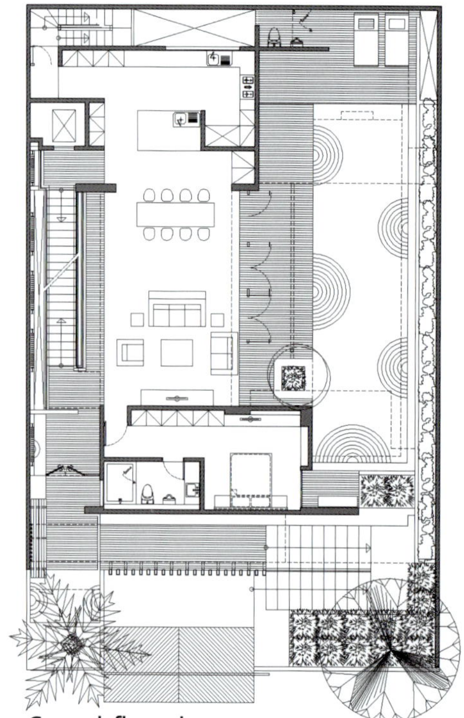

Ground-floor plan

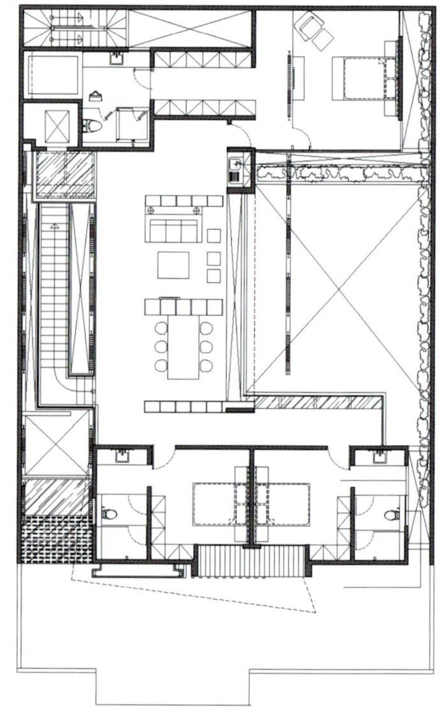

First-floor plan

In contrast to the openness of the interior space, the façade appears more solid and exclusive. Facing west, the house has been designed with a modified form of roof, which appears to extend to the front of the house. Made from a metal plate, this feature induces an eclectic feeling, while acting as a sunscreen and decorative element.

A combination of the client's two favourite materials—wood and marble—have been used for exterior walls and create a luxurious atmosphere. Two openings in the center of the façade allow the family to interact with the outside space, while an overhang frame maintains exclusivity. The solid façade is a response to the home's crowded surroundings. Aside from the functional aspects, the façade is an expression of the client. The façade also gives the home a distinct identity and fulfills the client's desire for an explorative design.

Middle: A hallway built with an aluminum pergola acts as a mode of transition from outdoor space to indoor space. **Bottom:** The continuous concept is applied in each transition element to achieve a spacious feeling. **Opposite:** The solid façade with its asymmetric roof dramatizes the house's appearance.

Site Area: 4306 ft² (400 m²) **Floor Area:** 8611 ft² (800 m²) **Photographer:** Fernando Gomulya **Design Period:** 2012 **Construction Period:** 2012–2014
Design Principal: Gerard Tambunan **Interior:** Agus Gunawan **Landscape:** Kiki (Sanggar Kemuning) **Contractor:** PT Dimigo Pratama
Structure: Ricky Theo **M&E:** PT Dimigo Pratama **Lighting:** Liam Sak Khian

Bob Kamei's House

Denpasar, Bali

Arte Architect & Associates

Inspired by architect Ketut Arthana's own dwelling, The Tree House (page 230), the client wanted a similar design for his own home. The site is located close to a river and tucked away from the hustle bustle of Denpasar city. This enabled the architect to incorporate a sense of tranquillity into the design, as wished by the client.

Nestled into a sloping hillside, the house adjoins a river and forest. Upon arranging the space, the architect utilized the land's contours to create different levels of space with varying degrees of privacy. The road's surface is the highest point of the site and became advantageous when creating additional private spaces on the lower level, all of which are surrounded by breathtaking scenery.

A reception area, located on the same level as the road, was designed as a narrow and slightly dim space with a bridge over a fishpond. Mossy Paras Silakarang stand stones were the main material used in the construction of the reception area. The space's brooding nuance was intentionally created as a prelude to entering the bright house.

Left: A multitude of openings in the house create bright indoor spaces and allow the occupants to enjoy the outdoor scenery.

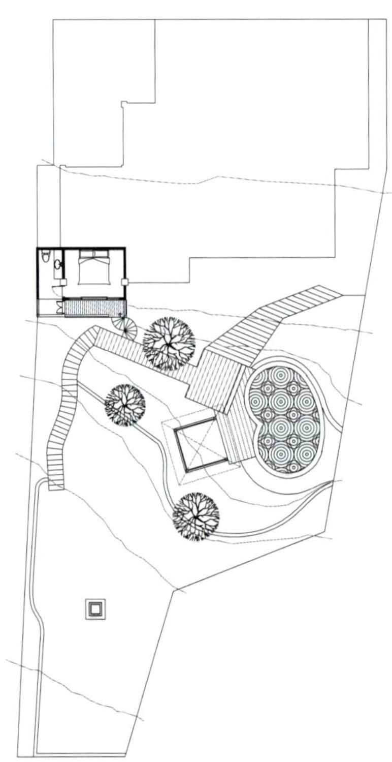

Ground-floor plan

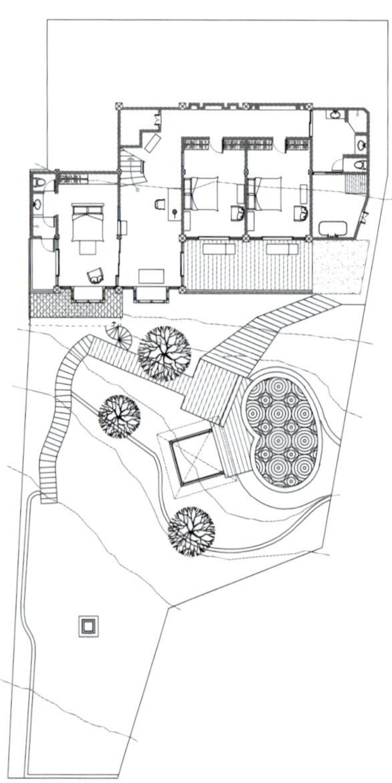

First-floor plan

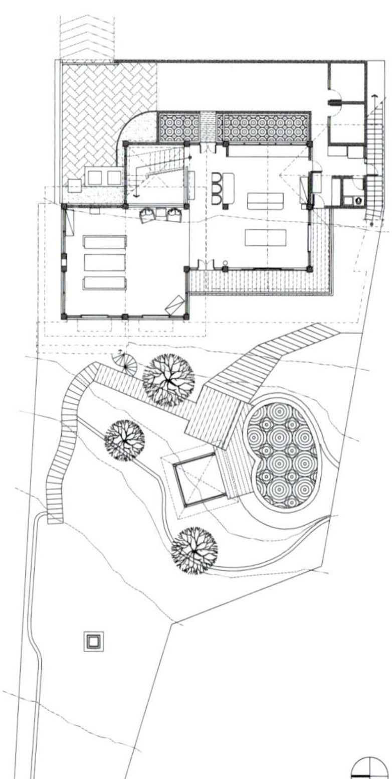

Second-floor plan

Bob Kamei's House

Opposite top: The terrace at the back of the house has the best scenery and provides a private and tranquil space. **Top:** Large openings have also been applied to the bedroom, creating an ultimate connection with nature when occupants are resting. **Bottom:** Some space functions have been designed as 'open but enclosed' through the application of openings on the ceilings and walls.

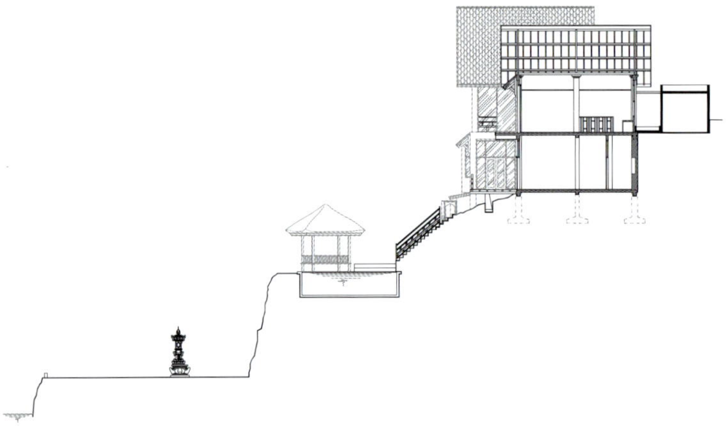

Transverse section

Bottom: Harmonious blends of natural materials on the house itself as well as the outdoor area echo the warm tropical climate. **Right:** In the living room, the architect applied a high, vaulted roof to expose the roof structure and glass openings. This creates a sense of spaciousness. **Opposite:** A view of the house from the river located at the lowest part of the site. Lush trees appear to cover the house.

In line with the client's wish, the architect designed the highest floor as a public space that holds a kitchen, dining room, and living room. Large windows and a high roof without ceilings make the area feel spacious and abundant with light. Equipped with sliding windows that can be opened widely, the occupants enjoy scenery of the bamboo forest and giant trees surrounding the site as well as the sound of the flowing river.

While the second floor has been allocated as a public space, the floors below have been designed for privacy. The bedrooms are located on the first floor and enjoy large river-facing openings, enabling occupants to engage with nature while indoors. The home's lowest level boasts the best natural scenery. A pool and bale *bengong* (a Balinese thatched-roof pavilion) surrounded by large trees create an idyllic outdoor space.

The abundance of natural scenery and the secluded location played an important role in achieving a sense of tranquillity within and around the home. These serene characteristics further support the home's purpose as a place of relaxation.

Site Area: 7965 ft² (740 m²) **Floor Area:** 5473 ft² (508.5 m²) **Photographer:** Sonny Sandjaya **Design Period:** 1998–1999 **Construction Period:** 1999–2000
Design Principal: Ketut Arthana **Structure:** Arte Architect & Associates

Brawa House

Canggu, Bali
Das Quadrat

Nowadays, Bali is not only a popular tourist spot, it is a place in which people choose to permanantely reside. The island appeals to those in other areas of Indonesia as it offers an esape from the bustling metropolitan cities and provides an environment closely linked to nature. Despite its increasing popularity, the owners of the House in Brawa sought to find a secluded site surrounded by nature upon which to build their home. The house is surrouded by rice fields and located in Umalas, Canggu—an area that still emodies Bali's natural beauty.

The architects were faced with a challenge when trying to achieve a scenic view of the rice fields. The west-stretching orientation of the fields meant that the harsh afternoon sun would have to be taken into consideration upon designing the home. Fortunately, two large trees—which are considered sacred in Balinese culture—stand tall at the edge of the fields, reducing the amount of heat that enters the site. Beneath the trees is a place for family praying.

The rice fields were fundamental when deciding on the layout of the building mass. The L-shaped design faces the rice fields at the back of the site. Hedges planted to border the site also ensure a constant view of the landscape.

Left: The living area is exposed to the pool terrace and separated with folding glass doors.

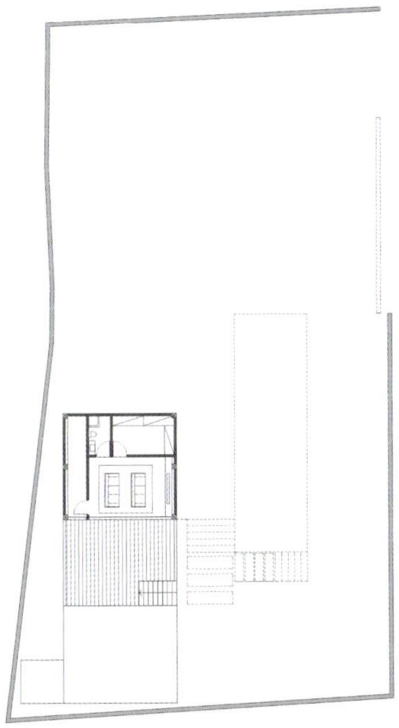

Ground-floor plan

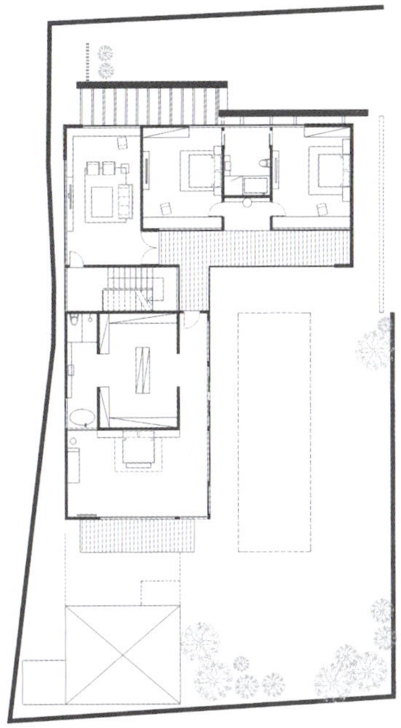

First-floor plan

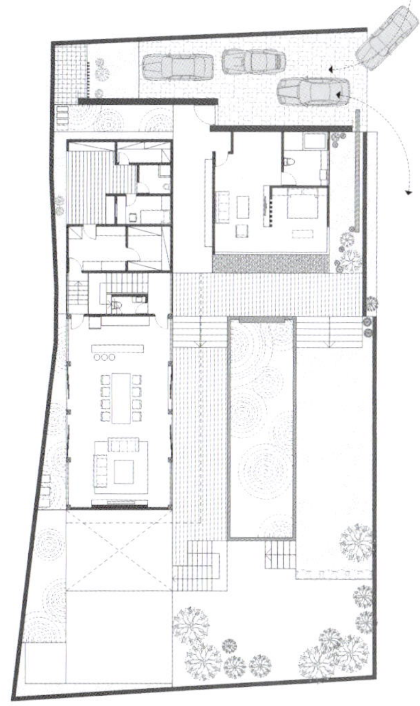

Second-floor plan

Opposite: Greenery was an integral element in the endeavor to create a building that adapted to the surrounding nature. **Bottom:** Transparent design in the living room is achieved by glass walls and doors, which blur borders between inside and outside.

Bottom: The dining room space is combined with the pantry. From here, occupants are provided a refreshing view toward the pool terrace. **Opposite top:** The rooftop area functions as a garden and private gallery. It is the perfect place to enjoy the serenity of nature. **Opposite bottom:** Occupants are able to enjoy a relaxing view of the surrounding greenery from the master bedroom, creating the sensation of resting completely within nature.

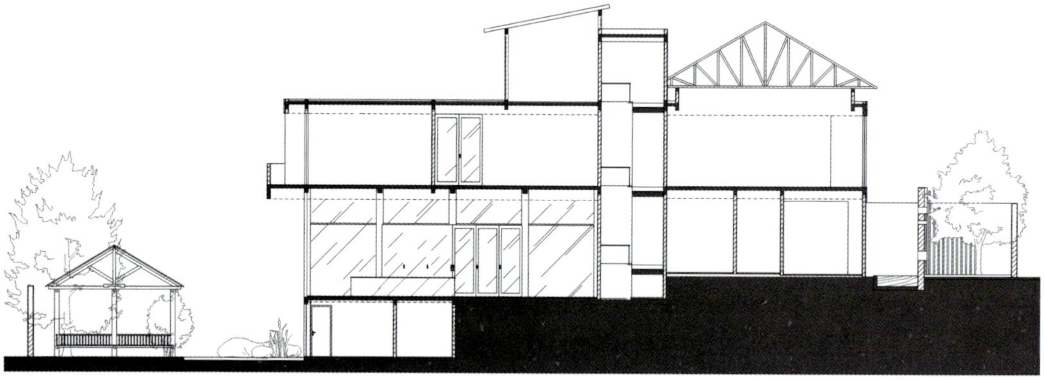

Section

Site Area: 8611 ft² (800 m²) **Floor Area:** 7535 ft² (700 m²) **Photographer:** Sonny Sandjaya **Design Period:** 2009 **Construction Period:** 2012–2014 **Design Principal:** Aditya Tan **Design Team:** Ardhian **Interior:** Das Quadrat, owner **Landscape:** owner **Contractor:** SFconstruction **Structure:** SFconstruction **M&E:** Das Quadrat **Lighting:** Das Quadrat

The spatial arrangement of the home has been tailored specifically to the occupants. The owners (husband and wife), their two children, and the owners' parents. The living room, dining room, pantry, and service area, as well as the parents' bedroom, are located on the ground floor. All of the rooms have been designed to face the pool. The main bedroom and the children's bedrooms are located on the upper floor. A private gallery occupies the space of the top floor.

The home has been designed to merge with nature. A transparent design has been applied through the use of glass walls and doors, which blur the border between inside and out. An extended vista gives the occupants a strong sense of the surrounding nature, even when inside the house. Wooden materials have been used for most of the buildings finishes, creating further harmony with the surrounding landscape.

BRG House Dago Bengkok

Bandung, West Java

Tan Tik Lam Architects

BRG House was designed by Tan Tik Lam and is located in Dago Bengkok, Bandung. The clients had no specific requests so the architect was given free reign to design the house. Having this freedom as well as a 5-acre (2-hectare) site to work with allowed the architect to focus the design on capturing the spectacular scenery. As a result, the home sits at the very edge of a cliff and enjoys unobstructed views of a beautiful valley.

Of the total land area, only about three percent was built on, with the rest left for future development of green areas. The house itself is located on the eastern side of the site—the furthest point from the outermost perimeter—and hidden within lush greenery. A paved path grants access to the home from the site's perimeter. Although a long walk, this path provides residents and guests with an interesting access point through lush trees and open green spaces.

The house comprises two building masses. There are no defining features that indicate an entrance, only a roofed terrace, which follows the shape of the building, and a reception area located in the east-facing building. Situated next to the swimming pool at the edge of the valley, this unhindered space allows residents to enjoy the wide and lush valley beyond.

Left: The swimming pool located at the very edge of the valley provides a unique living sensation.

Aside from the terrace and swimming pool, which are main features of this part of house, the building also holds non-private areas such as the parlor, dining room, and kitchen. Like the first building mass, the second mass has also been designed horizontally but built perpendicular to the first. The second mass consists of two levels: the basement level, which is reserved for service areas, and the ground level, which houses the bedrooms and study. Both masses are connected on both the inside and outside by steps and a ramp.

A cut-and-fill technique was employed during the construction process for stretched out sections in high areas. Heavily spread Strauss piles were applied to support the elongated building. Due to risks associated with ground movement, the structures of the house and swimming pool have been separated by dilation.

This method ensures that the structures do not disturb one another should ground movement occur. The home not only takes full advantage of its picturesque surrounds but also demonstrates considered, long-term safety for its residents.

Top: The continuity of the building mass continues on to the terrace. **Bottom:** Terracotta paint applied on the rough stone walls conveys a sense of warmth and earthy nuance to the cool white paint that dominates the house. **Opposite:** Square glass blocks in various sizes adorn the walls of the hallway ramp that connects the first and second building masses.

1 Drying area
2 Lounge
3 Maid
4 Bathroom
5 Kitchen
6 Storage
7 Carport
8 Fitness
9 Lavatory
10 Terrace
11 Dining room
12 Living room
13 Pool
14 Study
15 Bedroom
16 *Wudhu* (prayer preparation space)
17 *Musholla* (congregational space)
18 Wardrobe

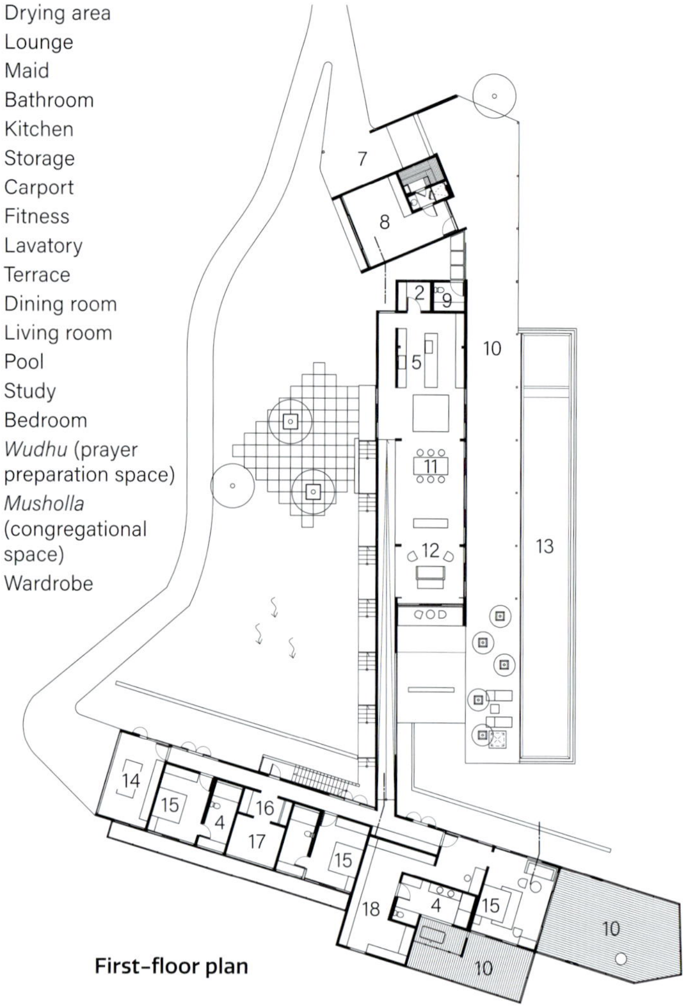

First-floor plan

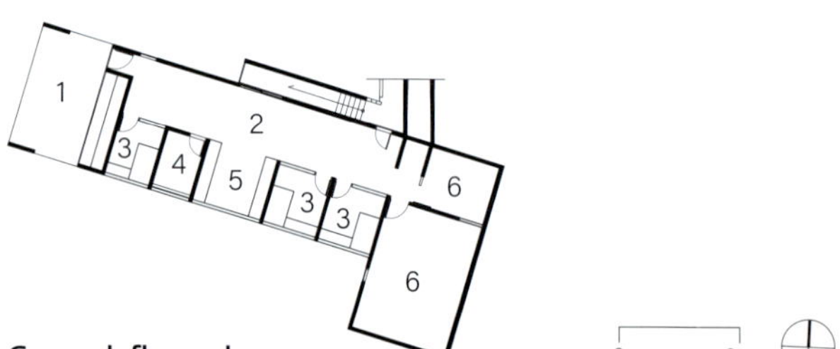

Ground-floor plan

Top: More than 90 percent of the lot has been left as green areas with preserved contours. **Middle:** The main feature of the house is the east-facing terrace and swimming pool, which are perfect for relaxing. **Bottom:** One of the architects' responsibilities to the environment was to refrain from cutting down existing trees. Instead, they were included as a part of the design. **Opposite bottom:** Sliding glass doors never fail to bring outdoor panoramas into the interior of a home.

BRG House Dago Bengkok

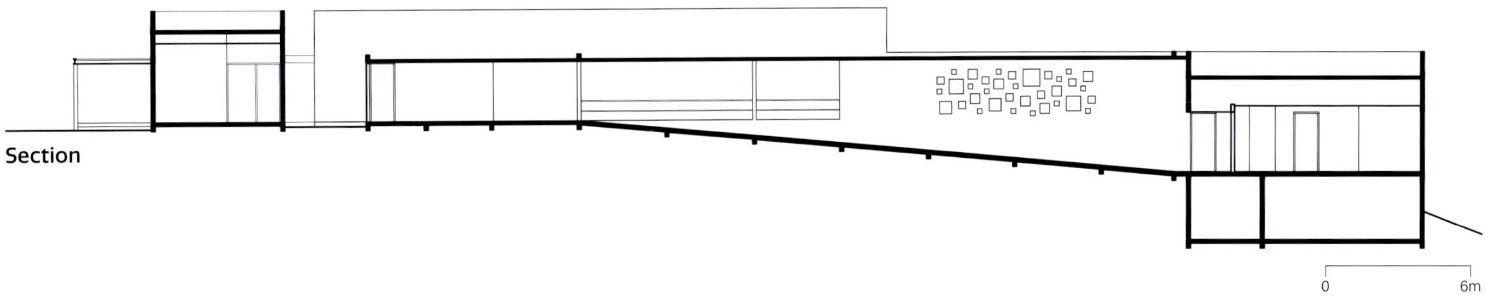

Section

Site Area: 215,278+ ft² (20,000+ m²) **Floor Area:** Ground floor: 1711 ft² (159 m²) First floor: 6028 ft² (560 m²)
Photographer: Sonny Sandjaya **Construction Period:** 2014 **Design Principal:** Tan Tik Lam

BTR House

Tangerang Selatan, Banten

Han Awal & Partners Architects

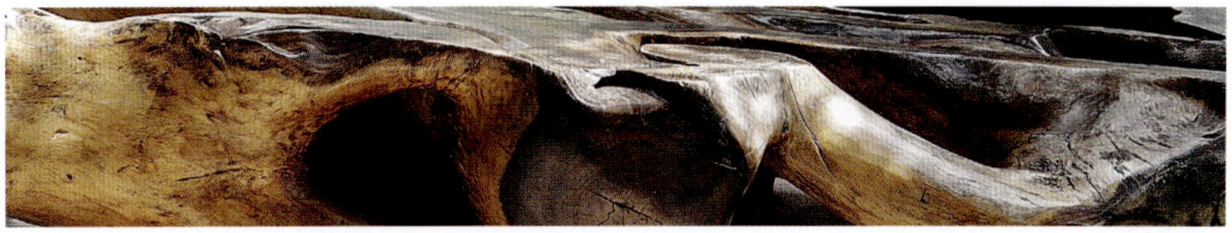

BTR House occupies only a quarter of an 8611-square-foot (800-square-meter site), with most of the area spared for open spaces. Yori Antar's private residence conveys his wish for a dwelling surrounded by greenery. By making use of basic tropical house principles and incorporating vernacular elements into the design, he has achieved an exemplary residence with nature as an essential component.

A wall of lush greenery creates an element of surprise upon entering through the home's solid metal gate. The carport is also surround by a dense vertical garden. The home's two main wooden doors are hidden beneath a plantation layer and provoke a sense of entering into thick woodlands. Fishponds located behind the vertical garden further enhance the natural atmosphere of the home's entrance.

Left: Hidden between the thick vertical garden is the main door of the house, giving a mythical experience as if entering a temple in a jungle.

An indoor corridor of white stucco and light grey tiles creates a sense of calm before leading out into more greenery. Wide sliding glass doors offer an extensive view out to a surprisingly vast courtyard adorned with the vivid greenery from various plantations.

This far-reaching courtyard space connects the family room at the back of the house and studio at the front. Broad glass openings provide sufficient natural air ventilation, allowing cool and comfortable breezes to circulate throughout indoor spaces.

The house subtly invites occupants to directly interact with the outdoor space. More than just an estuary for flora, the courtyard also functions as a space for activity. Couches placed in the outdoor area act as an extension of the family room.

Top: A spacious area on the second floor acts as a multifunctional room. Rattan has been used to cover the ceiling, giving a unique identity to the house. **Bottom:** The lounge area surrounded by greenery acts as a space away from the busy urban environment. **Opposite top:** Wide sliding doors at the family room blur the boundary between the inside room and its semi-outdoor extension space. **Opposite bottom:** A view from the studio room toward the open courtyard is framed by hanging plants. This emphasizes the tropical feeling of the house.

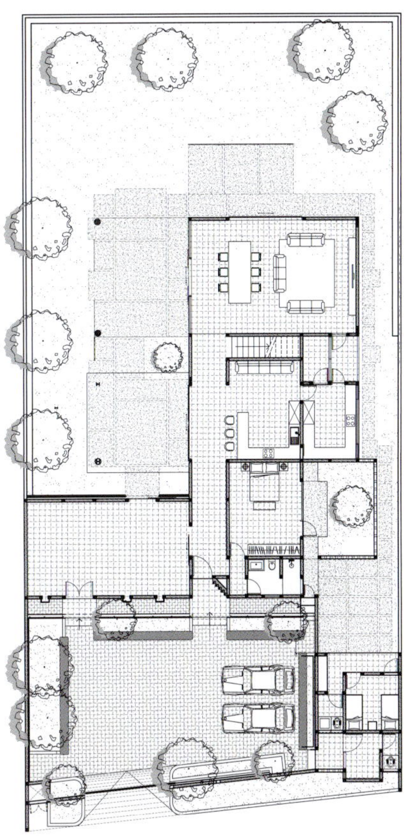

Ground-floor plan

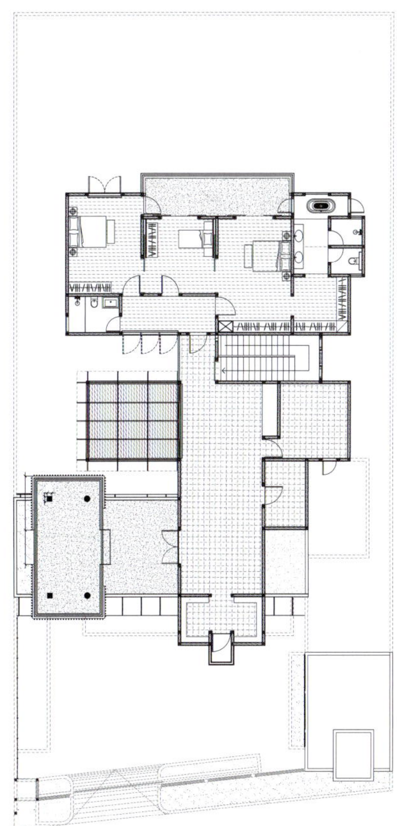

First-floor plan

A broad table-cum-chair in the form of a giant tree trunk provides a space to mingle as well as a view toward the turf garden at the very back of the site. An extended roof protects these spaces from extreme tropical weather, providing comfort in the open.

In addition to the generous courtyard, the home also has many other extensive spaces intended for socializing. On the upper level a spacious multifunctional room continues to an outdoor area. It too has been designed to bring occupants closer to outdoor space. Located beside this space is a gazebo boxed with wooden slats, which has been deliberately positioned to offer a view of the carport's vertical garden and inner courtyard. It is an alleviating escape from busy urban life.

The traditional Indonesian *lumbung* house (traditional pile-built rice house) inspires the building's form. Its upper mass sits distinctly on top of the vertical garden, with shades that cantilever out from the front terrace. The gabled roof is similar to the arched roof of the *lumbung* house, with charcoal-colored roof shingles instead of thatches. A single door on the front face replicates the openings in a *lumbung* house.

The house celebrates the area's amiable climate by merging indoor and outdoor spaces. Its design allows occupants to remain intimate with natural elements, making it the perfect place to spend time relaxing.

Top: The outdoor seating space features a pergola and timber seats, bordered by a row of trees behind.
Bottom: A hanging gazebo acts as a gathering space.
Opposite: A spacious area on the second floor acts as a multifunctional room. Rattan has been used to cover the ceiling, giving a unique identity to the house.

Site Area: 8843 ft² (821.5 m²) **Floor Area:** 2164 ft² (201 m²) **Photographer:** Sonny Sandjaya **Design Period:** 2013 **Construction Period:** 2013–2014
Design Principal: Gregorius (Yori) Antar **Design Team:** Khairul **Interior:** Han Awal & Partners Architects **Landscape:** Ono Landscape, GreenPad, PT Tropica Greeneries
Contractor: PT Hanny Rancangbangun Abadi **Structure:** Muchamad Umar **M&E:** PT Hanny Rancangbangun Abadi **Lighting:** Hadi Komara & Associates

Bukit Sadewa House

Semarang, Central Java
MSSM Associates

Bukit Sadewa House is located in the highlands of Semarang, which is colloquially known as Kota Atas (Upper City). The site is situated on a corner of a street in a housing complex, with its eastern side sitting adjacent to a slope. This location commands a full 180-degree view of Semarang City. The house is orientated to take advantage of this view.

Two passageways grant access to the house, one on the west side and another on the east side. The passageway on the east is the more formal of the two. Guests pass through a square concrete 'gate,' which frames the view of the city. Beyond this gate, they are welcomed by a wide expanse of gently contoured grass lawn, which covers the entire lot. A wooden deck adorns this area of the house (the front yard).

The lot itself is a thin strip of land on which the configuration of the house's layout is based. The 24-by-108-foot (7-by-33-meter) project was designed as a compact one-story house with a mezzanine and no permanent interior walls, except for the bedrooms and den. The pantry, dining room, and living room are all connected in one continuous layout.

Left: The fluid connection between the exterior and interior allows inhabitants to enjoy the excellent view from inside the house.

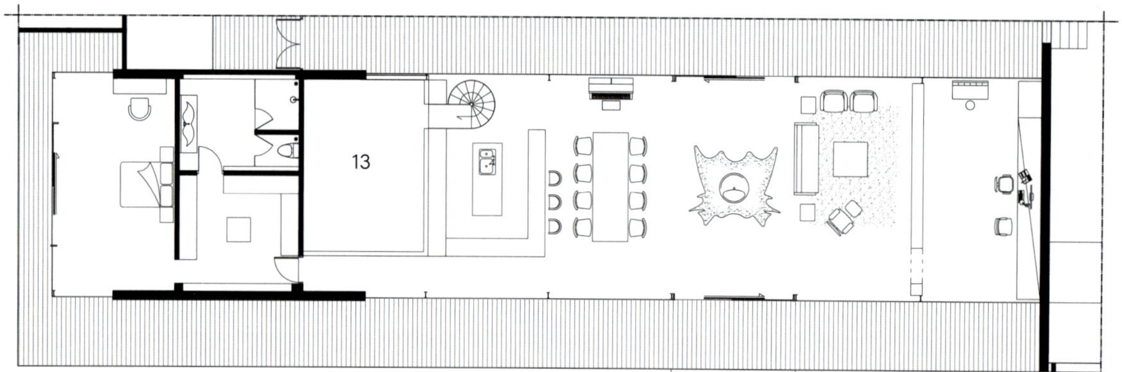

Mezzanine floor plan

1. Wood deck terrace
2. Foyer
3. Back terrace
4. Living room
5. Dining room
6. Pantry
7. Working room
8. Children's bedroom
9. Children's bedroom
10. Master bedroom
11. Walk-in closet
12. Master bathroom
13. Mezzanine

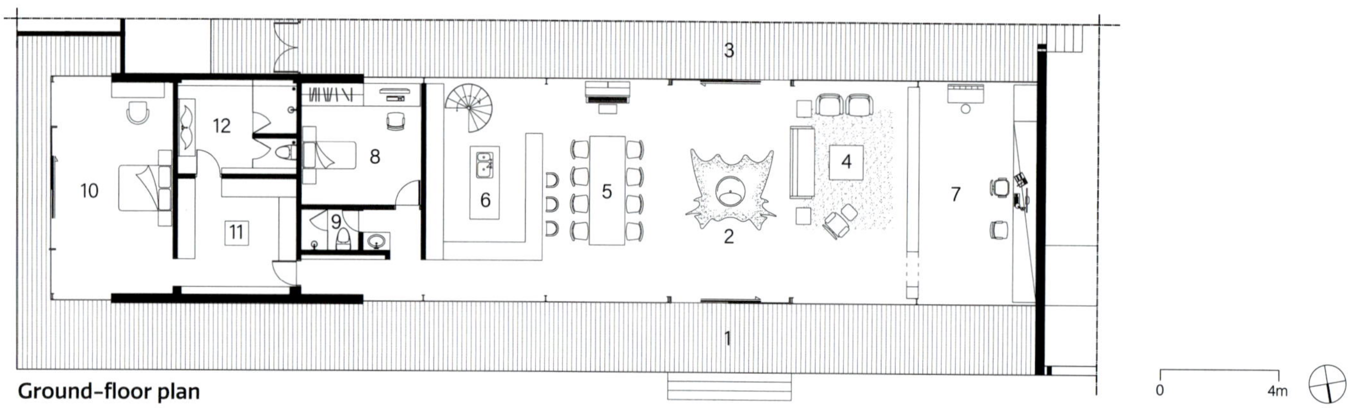

Ground-floor plan

In addition to its spatial arrangements, the view around the lot also shapes the appearance of the house. The longest side of the house is oriented to the east and west, with the east side directly facing the cityscape beyond the slope. In order to take advantage of the view from the interior, the house has been covered mostly with glass walls, which open and close so occupants can enjoy the fresh highlands air. These glass walls serve as a visual medium through which to enjoy the unparalleled view of the cityscape of Semarang, but also as a means of natural lighting, which makes the house appear wide, open, and buoyant.

Due to the site's hard and rocky ground, the house sits on a simple stone foundation. On the northern side of the lot a retaining wall to holds the ground and acts as a divider between the site upon which the house is built and another site located on higher ground. In spite of its solid terrain, the house at Bukit Sadewa balances modern design lines with architectural fluidity, making it a striking dwelling at the peak of Semarang City.

Opposite bottom left: The modern gateway above the house's entrance frames the panorama beyond. **Opposite bottom right:** Consistent with the warm tone of the materials, a brick wall serves as a backdrop for the family's activities and memorabilia. **Top left:** A row of wooden ceiling supports adds texture to the interior space of the house. **Top right:** With windows facing the sunrise in the east, the dining area is a perfect place to relax and enjoy the morning light.

Opposite: The retaining wall, lined with a row of bamboo plants, also functions as the divider between this house and the higher neighboring lot. **Below:** This house stands on a lot adjacent to a slope, surrounded by greenery.

Site Area: 9924 ft² (922 m²) **Floor Area:** 2390 ft² (222 m²) **Photographer:** Sonny Sandjaya **Design Period:** 2011–2012 **Construction Period:** 2012–2014 **Design Principal:** Revano Satria **Design Team:** Ina Setiawati, Aurelia Angela, Stephanie Nastasya **Interior:** Revano Satria, Aurelia Angela, Stephanie Nastasya from Revastudio **Landscape:** MSSM Associates **Contractor:** RSI Group **Structure:** Graha Garda Depan **M&E:** Flux Home **Lighting:** Flux Home

C5 House

Bogor, West Java

Tan Tik Lam Architects

During the Dutch occupation, Bogor was known as *Buitenzorg*, which means a place to relax. Owning a vacation home in Bogor was a dream for many Jakarta citizens seeking a calmer atmosphere. Although Bogor is becoming increasingly crowded, the interest in owning a vacation home in the area remains.

C5 House not only escapes the city crowds, it is completely secluded by woodlands. The architect was assigned to design a private villa on a site with an area of almost 1.25 acres (half a hectare) in Megamendung. The villa stands on steeply contoured land with a slope of between 30 to 40 degrees. The site remains lush with wild vegetation—pines, ferns, areca palms, needlewoods, and clove trees—and is often thickly fogged. The sound of insects reverberates throughout the day and night, enhancing the jungle-like atmosphere. The basic building coefficient, set at a mere 20 percent at most, makes the villa appear as a small dot amidst the thick vegetation.

Left: Spatial requirements have been split into two building masses connected with an open terrace.

Second-floor plan

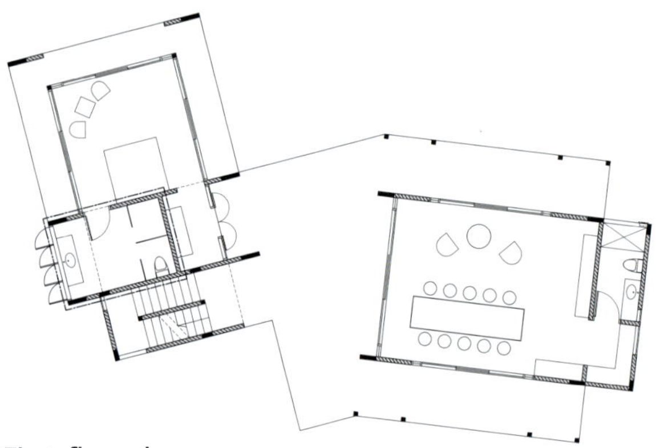

First-floor plan

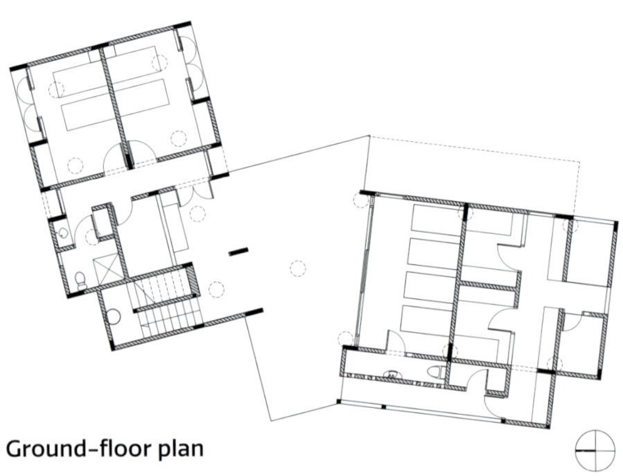

Ground-floor plan

C5 House

The architect designed the building to sit lower than the road. To reach it, a 108-foot-long (30-meter-long) ramp covered with concrete blocks leads residents to the parking area, from which they continue on foot across a wooden bridge. The long and interrupted circulation area forces occupants to interact with nature before entering the building. The villa itself stands vertically on stilts with bored pile foundation columns. The architect—who was committed to minimizing disruption of the site's natural condition—believed a vertical design would reduce direct contact with the ground. The foundations have been piled up to 36 feet (11 meters) into the ground to fully support the villa.

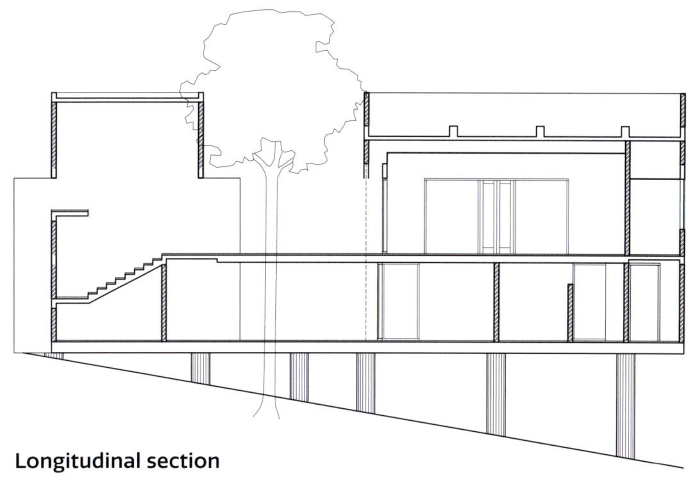

Longitudinal section

Opposite top right: To minimize the building's intervention on the ground, the villa is constructed as a house on stilts with a bored pile foundation. **Opposite bottom right:** The agathis dammaras tree that grows through the floors of the house. **Bottom:** The lush, green scenery of the valley and hills surrounding the villa imparts a calming effect to anyone who views it.

Designed as a three-story building, the villa possesses a neat visual expression; cubic shaped, made with concrete, and painted white. The spatial requirements have been divided into two masses with groupings based on floor level. The third floor, which is parallel to the parking area, acts as a break room consisting of stairways leading to the second floor. The second floor of the first building houses the main bedroom. The living room, dining room, and pantry are located in the second building. Communal bedrooms and a service area are located on the ground floor. In order to fully utilize surrounding views, large glass openings with sliding doors have been applied, allowing residents to enjoy the valley vista more freely. Although the building has been designed to encourage close interaction with nature, the occupants' comfort also had to be taken into consideration. Various ventilations equipped with insect screens and fans prevent rooms from becoming too damp.

In contrast to the roaring sounds of vehicles in more populated areas, the songs of insects incessantly fill the air surrounding the villa, providing occupants with a serene change in atmosphere. The C5 House is a beautiful escape from the routines of big cities.

Site Area: 41,473 ft² (3853 m²) **Floor Area:** 4370 ft² (406 m²) **Photographer:** Sonny Sandjaya **Design Period:** 2010–2011 **Construction Period:** 2011–2013 **Design Principal:** Tan Tik Lam **Design Team:** Priesto Naray, Maman Lesmana, Immanuel Chandra, Kelvin Lim, Aditya Budiarta **Contractor:** Pipih Priyatna Contractor Office **Structure:** PT Sentra Reka Struktur **Lighting:** Lighting Design & System

Opposite top: The wooden bridge that connects the parking area and the building. **Opposite bottom:** The neat villa, cubic shaped and painted in white. **Top:** The living room/ dining room located on the second floor of one of the building masses. **Bottom:** The bedrooms and outside corridors are granted views of tall trees and green hills.

Cipete_IH

Cipete, South Jakarta
Studio Air Putih

Enjoying the natural scenery is a limited privilege for those who live in big metropolitan cities. Aware of this challenge, Studio Air Putih introduced the client to an exclusive site with ample natural scenery. This modern and luxurious home sits on a vast site of 46,284 square feet (4300 square meters). In order to ensure occupant comfort, climatic consideration was essential to the home's design.

The house only occupies two-thirds of the site, leaving the rest of the area as green open space. Hidden behind the house, the vast site is enclosed by perimeter walls on three sides. Moreover, the open space can only be accessed from inside the house. This design approach enhances the home's exclusivity.

Left: Due to the incline of the ground, some rooms on the basement level, such as the meeting room, provide a view to the back of the house.

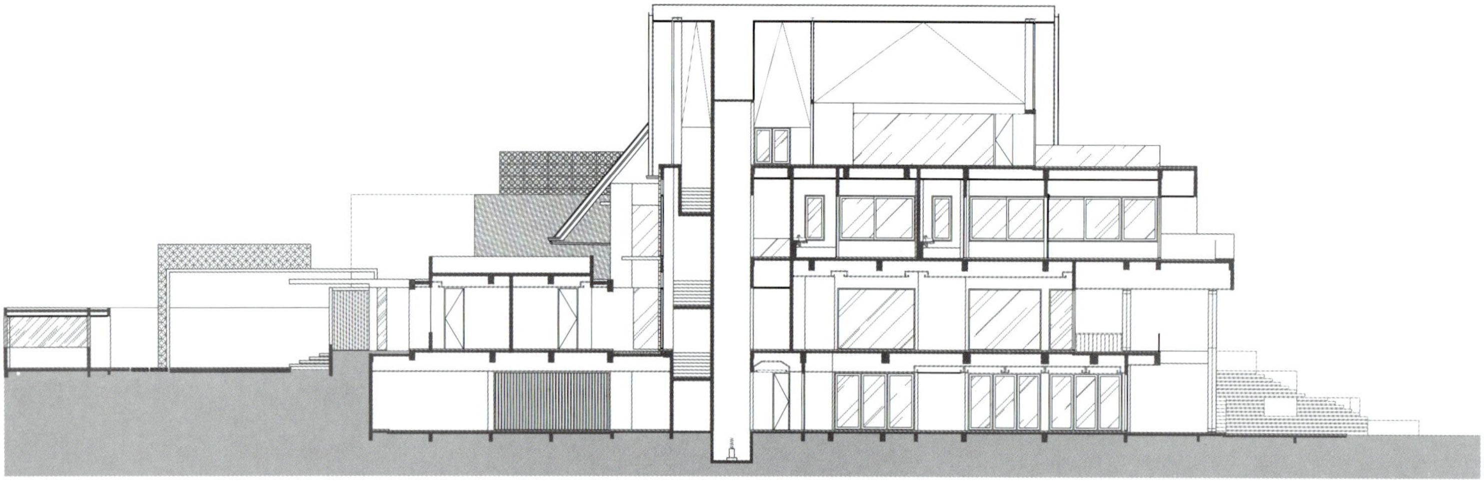

Section

To maximize the enjoyment of the open space, the house has been designed in a U-shaped plan, which opens to the back. A terrace fills the nook created by the home's layout. Here, occupants are able to directly interact with their natural surrounds.

Adjacent to the north mass, a lengthy swimming pool spans one side of the terrace and facilitates additional outdoor activities. A transitional zone between the turf ground and terrace has been designed to relate the different ambiences created by each area.

A set of stairs embellished by tall trees connects the open green space to the terrace on the higher level. This leads occupants through balanced elements of nature and man-made design.

The house has been designed to feel significantly open, which encourages occupants out into the natural environment. There are bedrooms on the north side and a living room on the east side. A dining room on the south side boasts a wide sliding glass door, which faces the terrace. The use of clear glass provides a broad view toward the refreshing greenery. When open, the glass doors blur the boundary between the inside and outside, while providing a soothing, tropical breeze. Through these openings, natural light can filter deep into the home's interior.

Left: Outdoor steps descend to the house's basement level and are bordered on one side by the lap pool.
Opposite: The living room has been designed as a void with a lofty ceiling. It is the most spacious indoor area.

Site Area: 46,285 ft² (4300 m²) **Floor Area:** 30,139 ft² (2800 m²) **Photographer:** Sonny Sandjaya **Design Period:** 2011–2012 **Construction Period:** 2012–2014
Design Principal: Denny Gondojatmiko **Design Team:** Willy Gunawan, Ragil Prayitna, Anindita Pamelaseli **Interior:** studio air putih **Landscape:** Hujanmas
Contractor: Sardjono Hadidjojo **Structure:** Arif Tonianto **M&E:** Jerry **Lighting:** Abdi Ahsan

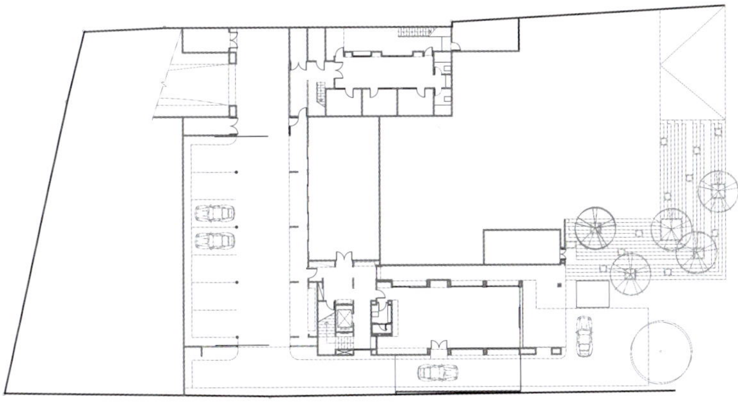

Basement floor Plan

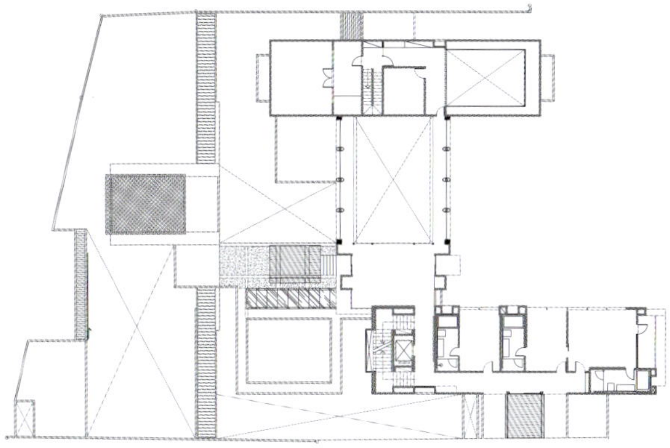

Ground-floor plan

The house is topped with high-pitched roofs, which emphasize its tropical aspects. However, instead of the typical 30-degree slope, the architect designed the roof with a 50-degree slope. This extreme slope, accompanied by the wide overhangs reaching up to 13-feet (4-meters) wide, make the roof the focal point of design. Following the shape of the high-pitched roof, a triangular, glass-walled chapel has been designed in the attic of the north side. The chapel's unique form and its topmost position deliver a signature design to the house. These speciality roofs not only contribute to a compelling exterior appearance but also create striking high ceilings within the home's interior—a design inspired by the upper-class Dutch houses from the colonial era.

Although the house incorporates many aspects of tropical house design, the architect has maintained its modernity. The façade showcases the use of cream-colored marble and dark natural stone as well as a dominant use of glass. The predominantly white and beige interior also successfully displays the home's modern and luxurious ambience.

Opposite: The dining room with high ceiling and wide glass sliding door offers a view to the terrace and garden. **Bottom:** The private chapel at the top level of the house showcases a distinct form with its wide overhanging roof and glass walls.

DRA House

Sanur, Bali
d-associates architect

The island of Bali is a well-known, go-to tropical getaway destination. The client, who lives a bustling city life, envisioned a home away from home for their family. D-associates realized this vision and designed a spacious home within a lush tropical sanctuary in Sanur, an upscale resort area and popular tourist haven. DRA House expresses a bold and dramatic exterior, while providing comfort and relaxation for occupants.

Before reaching the house, occupants experience a well-designed front yard and walkway bridge, which stretches over a pond. When crossing the concrete bridge, a solid wall of dark gray riverstones on one side and a green wall on the other offer a wholesome spatial experience. The journey to the entrance ends at a foyer topped by a flat wooden roof. The foyer, inspired by Bali's Aling-Aling Waterfall, acts as a transitional space before entering the home. The varying spatial sequences of the home's entrance allow residents to interact with nature. The indirect circulation also creates a sense of anticipation for the house itself.

Left: Due to the lightness of its enclosing elements and the absence of partitions, the living area on the ground floor merges with the outdoors.

Oriented toward a golf course, the two-story building has been separated into two volumes of space. These are located along the southern side of the site, creating plenty of open space on the north, with the pool and garden as the main focal points. The upper-level area comprises the family's bedrooms and bathroom. It appears as a slightly elevated box resting upon round concrete columns and shelters the lower-level area. This configuration allows the lower level to seamlessly blend with the surrounding environment and ensure fluid interaction as well as circulation for the family.

Top: The gable roof juts forward to shield the space from heavy tropical rain, while the bridge allows people to adore the view from a height. **Left:** The foyer marks the beginning of the sequential entrance toward the house. **Opposite bottom left:** A series of wooden jalousie windows can be opened, exposing the upper level to the outdoor surroundings. **Opposite bottom right:** An ornamental window acts as a decorative accent.

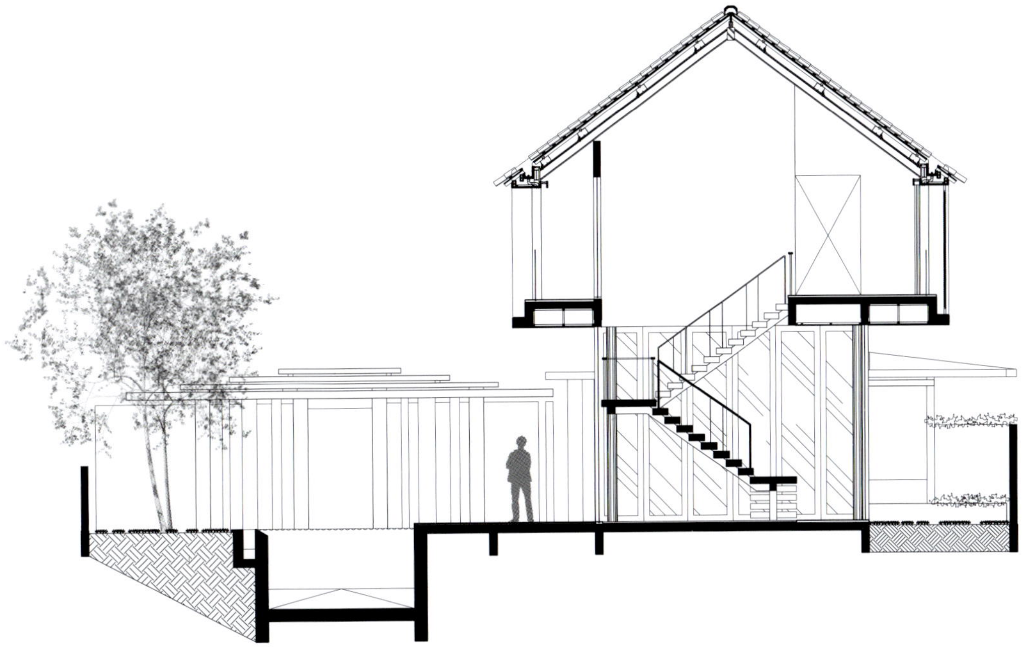

Transverse section

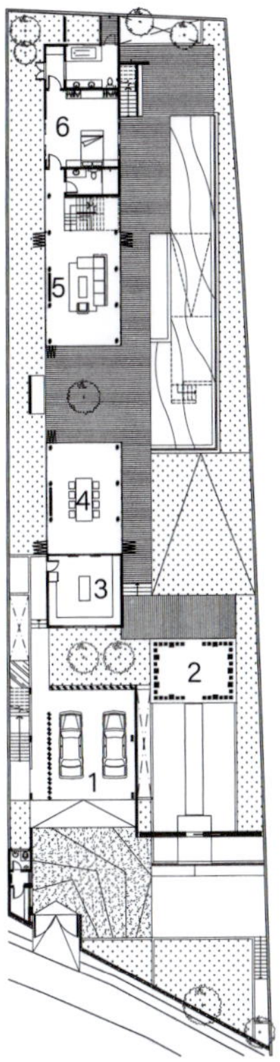

Ground-floor plan

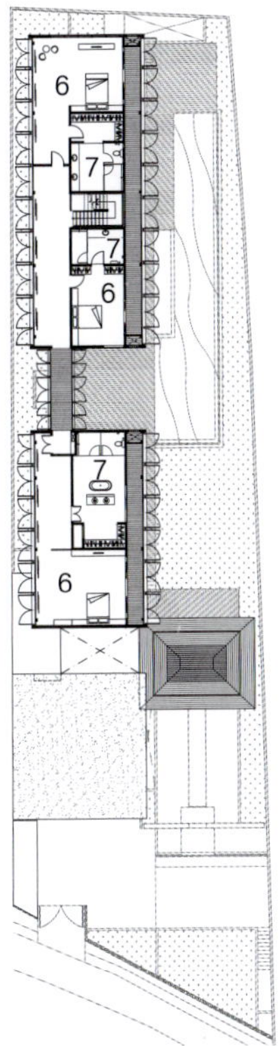

First-floor plan

1 Carport
2 Foyer
3 Kitchen
4 Dining area
5 Living room
6 Bedroom
7 Bathroom

0 5m

The home's design is embellished with distinct natural building materials of various textures and colors. The wooden bridge connecting the two main masses on the upper level is bordered by glass railing and shaded by a glass roof lined with wooden rafters. Heavy tones of dark-colored ironwood and plywood were chosen for the overall façade of the upper volume. Rows of hinged windows were installed along the north and south side of the upper volume's façade, providing adequate sunlight and cross ventilation. Folding glass doors on the lower volume span from the floor to ceiling. These doors open completely, transforming the ground level into one big continuous courtyard. This strategy amplifies a sense of lightness and openness, blurring the boundary between inside and outside, and toning down the home's solid composition. Natural materials have also been used at the entrance of the home. Recycled ironwood in irregular sizes encloses the foyer for a rustic outdoor accent. With a combination of local materials, intricate interior details, and a modern articulation of tropical architecture, the architect has successfully created a fitting holiday home that is at harmony with nature.

Opposite: The foyer marks the beginning of the sequential entrance toward the house. **Bottom left:** Due to the lightness of its enclosing elements and the absence of partitions, the living area on the ground floor merges with the outdoors. **Bottom right:** A walkway over a pond provides strong visual appeal for occupants and visitors.

Site Area: 13,746 ft^2 (1277 m^2) **Floor Area:** 9655 ft^2 (897 m^2) **Photographer:** Sonny Sandjaya **Design Period:** 2011 **Construction Period:** 2011–2013 **Design Principal:** Gregorius Supie Yolodi, Maria Rosantina **Design Team:** C. Kunti Dewanggani **Interior:** Sammy Hendramianto for Hadiprana **Contractor:** Paul Tendean (PT CKBP) **Structure:** Krisna Triadi **M&E:** Rusman Riady **Lighting:** d-associates architect

Gupondoro House

Bandung, West Java
APTA

Lembang is a district in the West Bandung regency. It is located 4921 feet (1500 meters) above sea level and surrounded by the lush and beautiful scenery of the Parahyangan Mountains. Due to the altitude and surrounding landscape, the weather in Lembang is noticeably cooler than the nearby city of Bandung. The area mainly consists of residential suburbs as well as many recreational areas. Houses within these areas are challenging to build. APTA's design of a studio house proves what is possible when nature becomes integrated with simple physics.

The owner who is also the architect conceptualized a house that would coexist with the surrounding landscape while taking advantage of Lembang's cool climate. Sitting on a 5382-square-foot (500-square-meter) site area, the four-story building was constructed using steel frames. The exterior is covered with a creeping plant and series of adjustable louver windows, which also operate as folding doors opening toward the balcony. This design strategy camouflages the house and draws attention to the landscape. It also creates obscured boundaries between the outdoor area and the interior as well as allowing natural sunlight and air to circulate throughout entire house. The use of steel frames was intended to make the house flexible for any future changes to materials or space functions. It also gives the house a weightless and airy aesthetic.

Left: Maximum openings throughout the house fully incorporate nature.

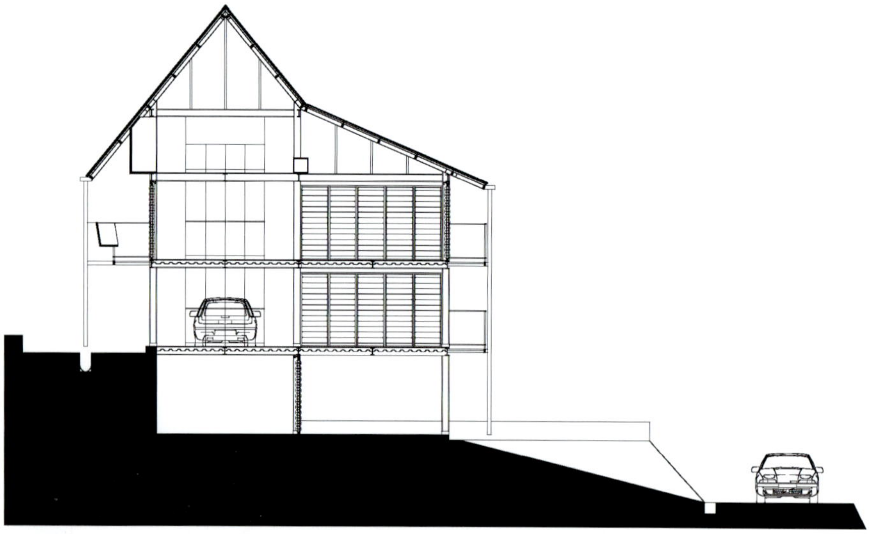

Section

The site's steep hillside required a significantly vertical design, which resulted in the division of living and private zones across multiple floors: The basement functions as the service and communal area; the ground floor as the meeting room; the first floor is used as a working area and is equipped with an outdoor sitting space; while the attic houses the owner's bedroom, which overlooks the studio. The home can be entered upon crossing an elevated bridge. The railing on both sides of the bridge is masked with creeper plants, creating a serene and beautiful entrance feature. The residual space beneath the bridge is shaded by the creeper plant and has been utilized as a parking area and open-air living space. Acting as a barrier between its neighbors, the architect decided to use a gabion wall made of stacked stone tied together with wire, as opposed to a solid-mass wall. Mirroring the steep side, the roof begins with a gable form then continues to slope downward, creating a connection with the contour of the landscape. The eaves then extend to protect the balcony and outdoor sitting space from the rain. Consequently, the interior has high ceilings. Not only does the roof provide relief from the hot air, it also makes the whole space seem larger.

Left: From a distance, the house portrays a contemporary residence nestled in the hills surrounded by untamed nature. **Opposite:** Maximum openings throughout the house fully incorporate nature.

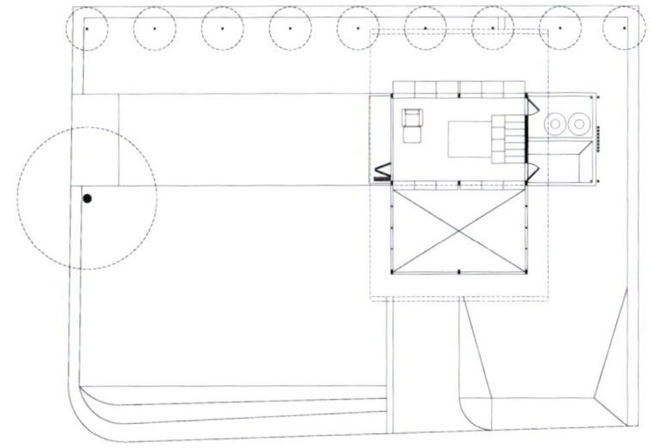

Attic floor plan

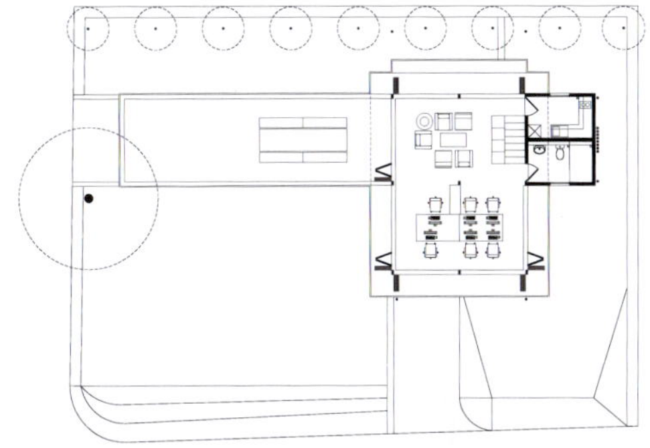

Upper-floor plan

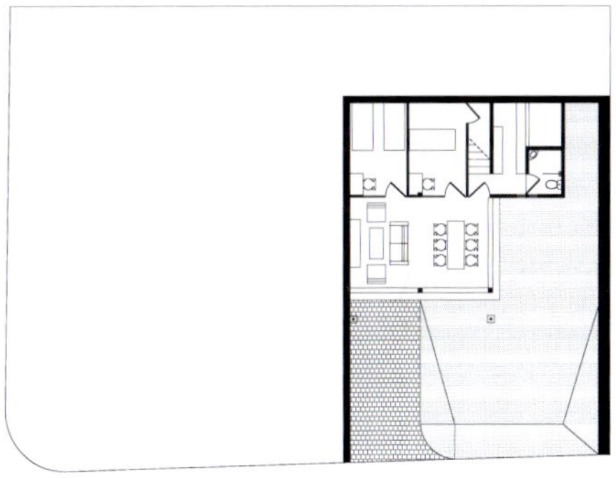

Ground-floor plan

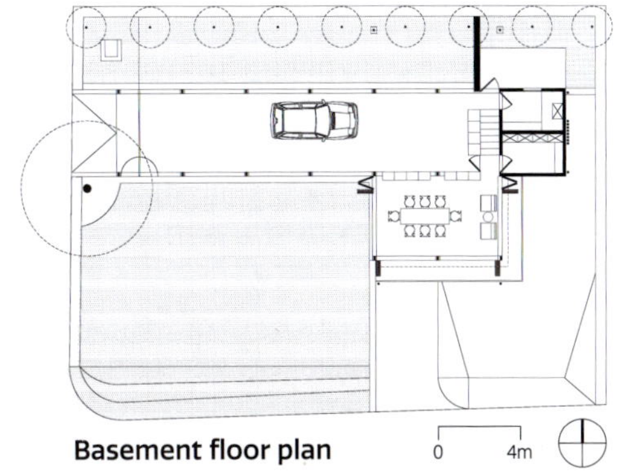

Basement floor plan

Gupondoro House

All of the home's interiors exude a rustic charm. The floors and parts of the walls are embellished with a combination of reused wood finishes, old tiles and furniture, most of which were obtained from a former Dutch Colonial house. These aesthetic touches create a cozy atmosphere within the home.

By maximizing openings to capture cool breezes, sun, and daylight, APTA have created a home that relates to its climate without impacting the natural landscape. The relationships among varying elements—structural, aesthetic, and natural—compose the simultaneously open and intimate space of Gupondoro House.

Opposite top left & left: The team opted for adjustable louver windows doubling as folding doors as an effective adaptation mechanism to control aeration and sunlight. **Opposite top middle, opposite top right & opposite bottom:** In contrast to its rugged exterior, the interior is welcoming with the application of wooden panels for walls, doors, and flooring. **Top:** From a distance, the home's relationship with the surrounding topography is further realized.

Site Area: 1640 ft² (500 m²) **Floor Area:** 827 ft² (252 m²) **Photographer:** Sjahrial Iqbal **Design Period:** 2012 **Construction Period:** 2013 **Design Principal:** Oky Kusprianto **Design Team:** Priyanto **Interior:** APTA **Landscape:** APTA **Contractor:** Joshua Alfasan **Structure:** Joshua Alfasan, Jimmy Paat **M&E:** Joshua Alfasan **Lighting:** APTA

Hanging Villa

Lembang, West Java
Wastu Cipta Parama

Hanging Villa was designed as a weekend getaway from the hustle and bustle of the city. It is located in Sindangwaas Village, between the cities of Bandung and Lembang. To gain access to the villa occupants must traverse a narrow and ascending dirt road. This landscape condition enables the village to retain its tranquility, as few motorized vehicles are able to navigate the difficult road.

The steeply contoured slope compelled the owner to create terraces in anticipation of potential landslides.

The architect realized that constructing a building on a steep slope would be far more expense than if the building were to follow the contours of the land. As a result, the building mass sits parallel to the slope on the even side of the site and is supported by a deep foundation. The architect also perfected the terraced plot by continuing the construction of retaining walls, which also function as the villa's exterior walls.

Left: The main building viewed from the terrace below.

Above: Frameless glass sliding doors successfully draw the outside scenery into the interior. **Opposite bottom:** The interior of the common room is dominated with wood-covered material, enhancing relaxing natural nuances.

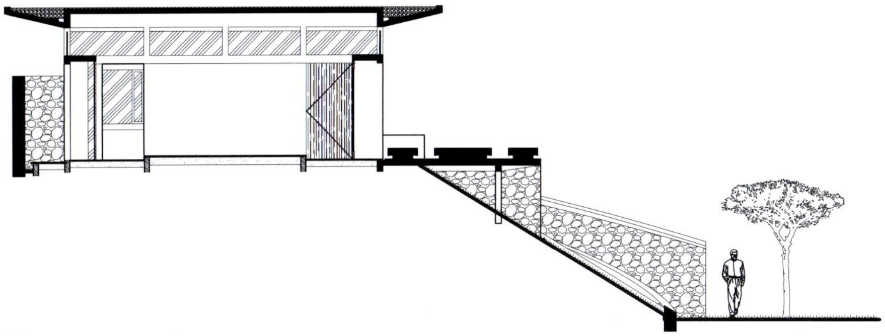

Transverse section

The basic building coefficient of the villa is around 20 percent, with relatively simple spatial needs: a master bedroom, two children's bedroom, and a common room. These spaces are housed within two one-story-building masses with linear layouts, which intersect perpendicularly. The 26-foot-high (8-meter-high) gap between the two masses creates an intermediary space, which functions as the common room. Several rooms have been designed to hang over the slope. This cantilever design enabled the architect to minimize changes to the contour of the land while increasing the occupant's relationship to the outdoors while indoors.

The simple shapes of the building masses are enhanced by the choice of the materials and colors: concrete, finished with white and gray paints. Concrete was chosen as the main material due to its durability and also because the architect deliberately wanted to create a simple and calm building expression. An elevated ceiling in the common room allows occupants to enjoy the surrounding scenery through a wide viewing range.

The building was designed to frame a picture of the landscape. The enchanting panorama of Bandung captured by the many frameless openings is the highlight of the home.

Top: The house is placed upon a steeply contoured slope, compelling the architect to create a terraced landscape. **Bottom:** Rows of trees soften the rigidly geometric expression of the building. These trees also act as the scenic backdrop seen from the direction of the villa. **Opposite:** The tree canopy and ceiling overstack shield outdoor areas of the house from bright sunlight.

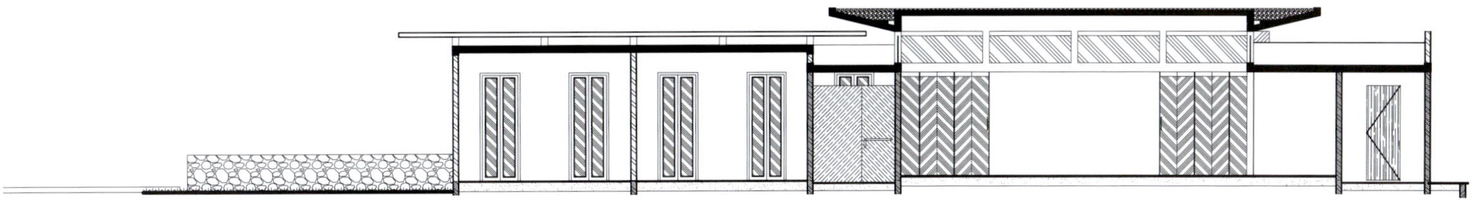

Longitudinal section

Site Area: 43,056 ft² (4000 m²) **Floor Area:** 2691 ft² (250 m²) **Photographer:** Sjahrial Iqbal **Design Period:** 2009 **Construction Period:** 2009–2010 **Design Principal:** Alex Santoso **Design Team:** Rizky Indraswuary, Astrid Naomi, Hegiasri **Interior:** Rachmat **Landscape:** Timmy & Christine **Contractor:** Pipih Priyatna **Structure:** Hermanto Subagyo **M&E:** Wastu Cipta Parama **Lighting:** Wastu Cipta Parama

Home in the Terraced Garden

Bandung, West Java

Sunaryo

Sunaryo, an Indonesian artist hailing from Bandung, once received an enormous piece of valuable timber as a gift. He believed the broad and heavy wooden slab to be of such high artistic value that he felt compelled to create a home for it on his personal land, located in the sloping terrains of Dago Giri in the city of Bandung.

This house was not originally intended to be more than a shelter for the wooden slab but upon further development Sunaryo determined that the slab could be used as furniture. The wooden slab was then crafted into an elongated table with accompanying raised-floor seating. By placing the table in a spacious room, it became the centerpiece of a home reaching a total of 861-square-feet (80-square-meters). Situated around this room is a bedroom, kitchen, sitting room, and veranda shielded with a woven bamboo pergola. The veranda has a walkway leading to Sunaryo's painting studio, which is separate from the main house.

Sunaryo based the design of the space between the house and studio on the land's natural contours. Gazebos, a swimming pool, and outdoor seats feature throughout the site, providing spaces to relax and enjoy the surroundings. By taking advantage of the contours, Sunaryo was able to create various terraces with different functions. These terraces connect to one another via outdoor stairs and stepping-stones.

Left: The wooden walkways are punctured to make way for existing trees.

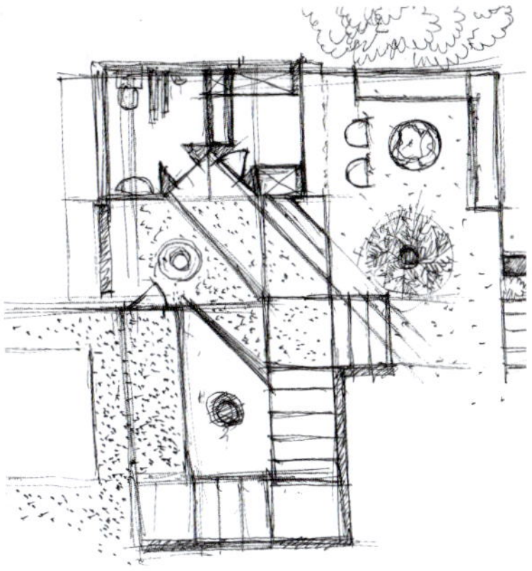

The garden features various tropical plants as well as ornamental plants, such as ferns, fountainbush, and heliconia, which are placed alongside the path and pools to add color and texture. In open areas, wide-canopied trees have been planted for shade. These natural elements, along with Sunaryo's sculptures, have been artfully arranged throughout the landscape.

Opposite: Enormous stones, sometimes sculpted by Sunaryo, have been placed along the garden as artistic landscaping elements. **Top:** The veranda is a showcase of locally sourced materials, accessories, and encompassing greenery. **Bottom left:** The contoured land has been designed as open-terraced spaces with distinct zones, but remain connected to each other. **Bottom right:** Sunaryo's design sketch of the tiered garden terrace.

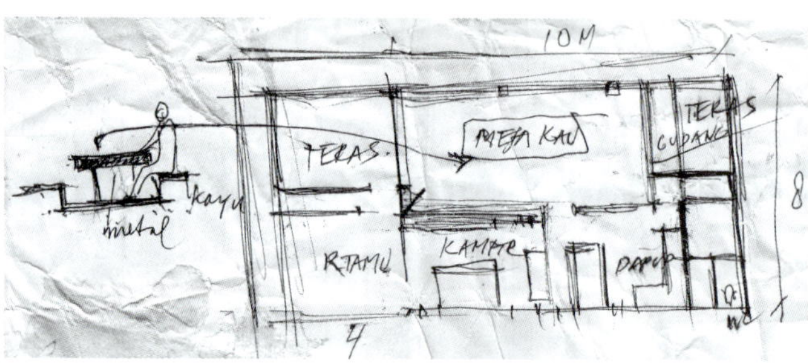

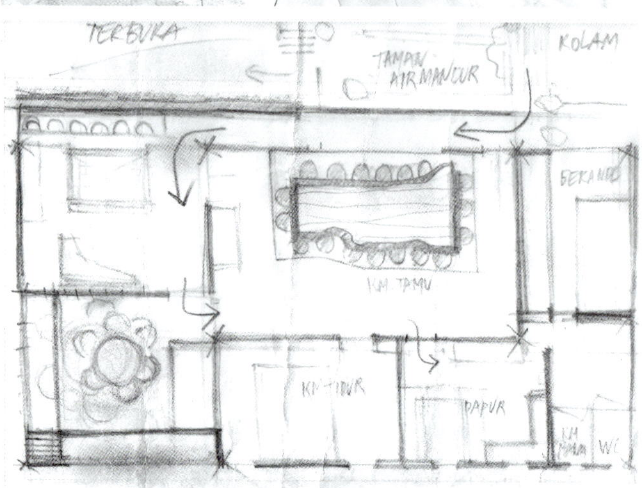

The main house features woven bamboo walls and is punctuated with many wide openings, which allow cool air to flow into the interior space. Aside from bamboo, natural materials such as wood and stone have been extensively used throughout the house. Sunaryo's artistic touch is further apparent in the home's finishing details with signature bursts of red paint applied throughout. Patterns in the specially woven bamboo partitions and pergolas have been exquisitely crafted and add further artistic value to the home.

Uniquely, Sunaryo conducted the home and landscape design organically and fluidly without working drawings. He communicated his designs to the construction workers in the form of sketches on spare papers, cigarette boxes, and on an enormous stone in the park while he observed the construction process. Even without an architectural background, Sunaryo's artistic expertise is highly apparent in the home's design, which naturally optimizes the contoured land into an exquisite dwelling.

Opposite top: The landscape design reduces the distinction between inside and outside spaces, resulting in a home that feels very close to nature. **Opposite bottom:** Sunaryo's design sketches upon flattened cigarette boxes, drawn while observing the construction with the workers. **Top:** The wooden slab is crafted into an elongated table to be used with floor seating. **Bottom left:** Various details of the crafted materials used throughout the house. **Bottom right:** In his paintings, Sunaryo characteristically uses precise elements of the color red to draw viewers' attention. The same principle applies to his design for the interior, as reflected in the subtle detail of the window bars.

Floor Area: 861+ ft^2 (80+ m^2) **Photographer:** Sonny Sandjaya

I+L Residence

South Tangerang, Banten
andramatin

The site is located on a residential area on the southwest outskirts of Jakarta city. Before it became a residential area due an increasing urban population, it was a dense palm forest. Fortunately, the site has retained its dense natural environment. Towering palm trees grow closely together, leaving only patchy open spaces. Eliminating existing trees is a common solution for many architects as it allows them design freedom. Andra Matin, however, takes an unconventional approach. Instead of removing obstructing trees, he uses them to guide the outcome of his design.

After assessing what patches of space were available throughout the site, he divided the house into several masses. Four cuboid masses are distinctly visible between the heaps of palm trees. Exposed-concrete panels have been used as exterior walls because they match well with the tones of the palm tree trunks and require minimal maintenance. Long and narrow windows grace the mainly solid surfaces of the building masses. In response to climatic conditions, concrete fins run vertically along the building to prevent excessive sunlight from penetrating into the home. They also disguise the windows to give the impression of a smooth and solid façade.

Left: A ramp guides people to the upper level, where the majority of rooms are located.

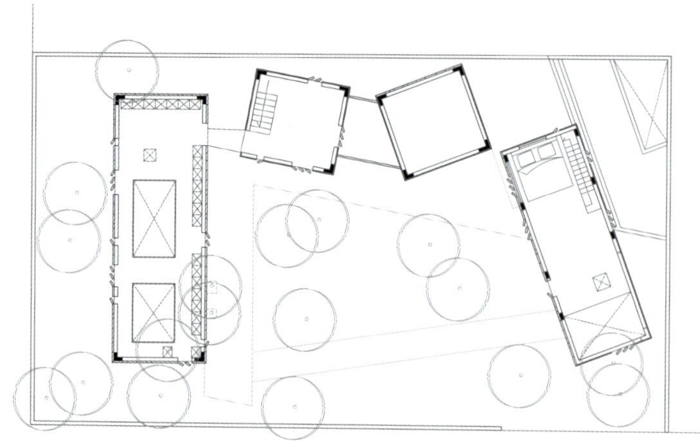

Second-floor plan

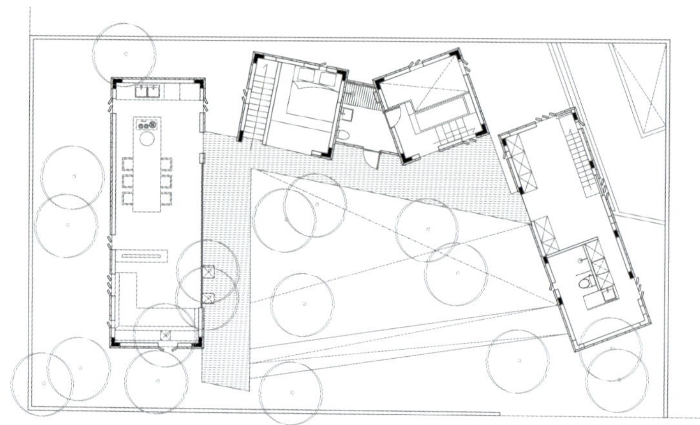

First-floor plan

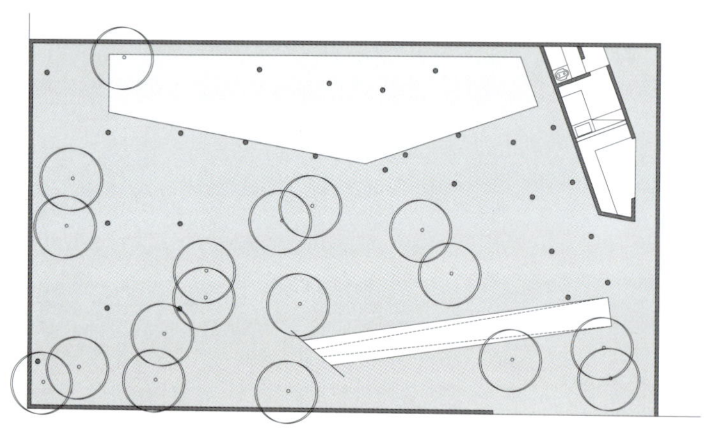

Ground-floor plan

Like many other of Andra Matin's works, surprise is an essential aspect in this home's design. Compared to its enclosed outward appearance, the ground level presents itself as an open outdoor space. By lifting the masses from the ground, he achieves a spacious arrangement of pilotis on the ground level. This area is used as the family's place for daily activity. A wooden table placed beneath the pilotis acts as a gathering place for dining or just enjoying the weather. It is protected by the shade of the upper mass. An inner court covered in jagged pebbles and soaring palm trees has been designed as the center of the house, with all the masses and open space on the ground facing the court.

Opposite left: The swimming pool is located below the floating mass.
Top: A walkway with a wall of slated wood connects each of the masses.
Bottom: The ground level consists of a xeriscaped inner courtyard and an open space for everyday activities.

Site Area: 4424 ft² (411 m²) **Floor Area:** 3003 ft² (279 m²) **Photographer:** Sonny Sandjaya **Design Period:** 2003–2015 **Construction Period:** 2015
Design Principal: Andra Matin **Design Team:** Ady Putra Sanjaya, Gana Ganesha **Interior:** andramatin, owner
Landscape: andramatin, owner **Contractor:** Alex Gandung **Structure:** Hadi Jahja **Lighting:** andramatin, owner

The pilotis replicate the site's palm trees and make it difficult to differentiate between nature and what is man-made. This achieves a sense of harmony throughout the home and site. The idea of merging the natural with the structural has also been implemented inside he home. Andra Matin made the bold design choice of fully incorporating the existing trees into the home's interior layout. As a result, the trees pierce through rooms and beyond the roof. In contrast to the gray tone of the exterior, light-colored teakwood has been used on the walls and ceilings of the interior. The teakwood gives the trees a subtle presence throughout the home.

The first mass of the house, which consists of a joint living room, dining room, pantry, and mezzanine level for a private library, includes two palm trees in the interior. At a first glance, the trees are difficult to recognize as they blend in with the room. One tree disguises itself as a column at the edge of the room. The other tree is located in the middle of the pool on the ground floor. It pierces through a hole in the dining table on the next level before reaching through the ceiling. An additional intruding tree is located in the mass that contains the master bedroom and bathroom.

A skylight in the form of an acrylic umbrella has been designed as a passageway for each of the palms inside the home. By incorporating the natural surrounds entirely into his design vision, Andra Matin has created a truly unique dwelling.

Opposite top left & opposite top right: The child's study room enjoys a view outside through a low glass window. **Opposite bottom:** Light-colored teakwood dominates the interior of the house and contrasts with the exterior space. **Top left:** The trees pierce through the interior. **Bottom right:** The mezzanine floor of the first floor with a palm tree that casually grows through the interior.

Inzaya House

Bandung, West Java
Pipih Priyatna Architects

For those of us who desire a dwelling with breathtaking views, a glass house perched on top of a hill would be a dream come true. A steeped hillside offers a sense of drama while panoramic views of ever-changing skies, natural landscapes, and distant city lights are a sight of constant fascination. This describes the context of the Inzaya House site in Bandung. It is perched among a cluster of hillside villas in the highlands of the city.

This weekend home was designed as a place to rejuvenate while gathering with friends and family. The site's astounding view, which is well away from the bustle of the city, was given primary consideration in the design. In order to optimize panoramic potential, the house is first and foremost oriented parallel to the view. The mass is elongated lengthwise to receive the widest possible opening against this view. Because higher grounds offer increasingly boundless sights, the topmost floor of the house has been designed as a gathering room, allowing occupants to enjoy the best possible panoramic view.

Left: Inzaya House showcases wide glass openings framed with steel structures on a steep slope.

Due to the isolated location of the site, occupant privacy was not a pressing issue during design. Transparency is welcomed from inside as well as outside. Floor-length curtains enclose the perimeter of the house but are usually swept aside. Wide glass panes, bordered in black metal encasement, are sandwiched between the floor plates of the ground and second floor. From a side view, the general appearance of the house resembles a framed box: a flat roof overlaps the entire mass to provide shade from intense daylight and is supported gracefully by a steel column at each corner.

If the house were located somewhere with a warmer climate, such as Jakarta, the enclosing glass windows and openings would cause the home to need air-conditioning. Fortunately, the highlands of Bandung have a cooler climate and this is not the case. Natural ventilation allows the home to remain perfectly cool, even during noon. A line of perforated steel panels, bordering flush against the second-level communal room, allow outside air to circulate from below.

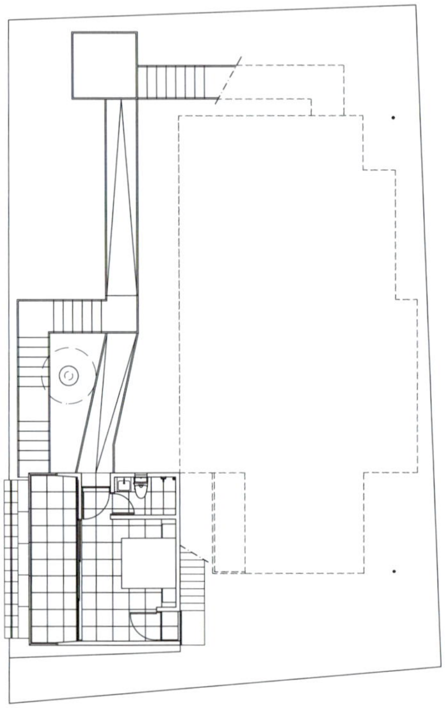

Mezzanine floor plan

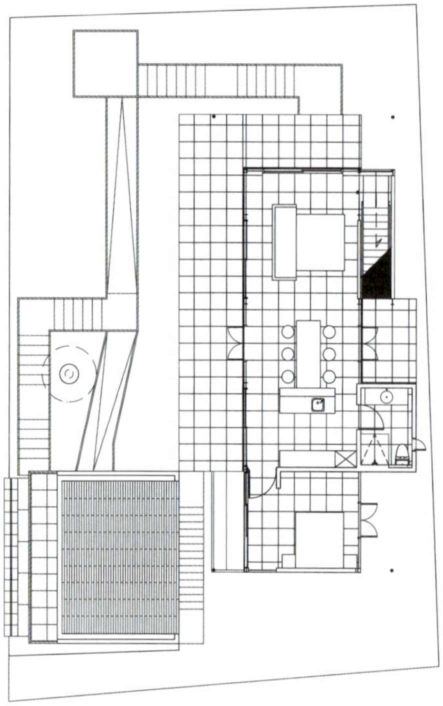

Ground-floor plan

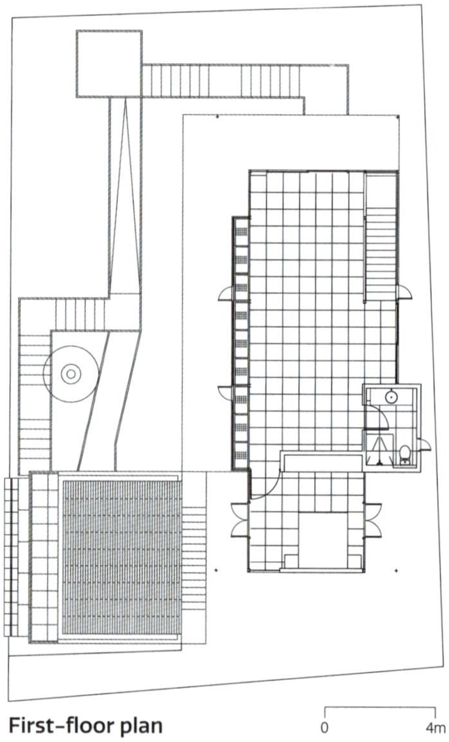

First-floor plan

Top: From the side, the house resembles a framed box with its wide overhanging roof supported by slim columns. **Opposite top:** The sitting room on the first floor provides a sweeping view of the sky and the contoured expanse ahead. **Opposite bottom:** On the second floor, the communal room opens up to a panorama of the hill and the steep slope. Perforated-floor panels allow outdoor air to circulate within the house.

Due to the strong gusts of air hillside regions are prone to, ventilation through large frontal openings has been intentionally avoided.

The hillside contour of the site inevitably informs the architecture of the house. Because the main road is located at the base of the slope, access by foot toward the house had to be designed in an ascending manner. This became especially relevant during the construction process, with materials and people travelling upwards. The architects decided on steel for the main structure, not only because it would maximize panoramic views but also because it is lightweight and easily assembled on steep ground.

Among the cluster of neighboring villas, Inzaya House's steel-frame appearance provides an interesting contrast. While nearby houses are largely built of white and gray concrete, this design consciously opts for darker, slimmer frames and glass openings, chosen as a response to its prime location. By understanding and optimizing the strengths of a hillside landscape and applying design solutions to the advantage of colder tropical areas, Pipih Priyatna Architects have created a wonderful adaptation of the glass-house typology.

Top: The seating area on the second level of the house reveals dramatic sights of the mountainous surrounds. **Left:** Leading up to the house, the wooden outdoor stairs are shaded by arching trees and tropical shrubbery. **Opposite:** At night, the glass house shines like a lantern amidst the lush surroundings.

Site Area: 4090 ft² (380 m²) **Floor Area:** 2551 ft² (237 m²) **Photographer:** Sonny Sandjaya **Design Period:** 2014 **Construction Period:** 2014–2015
Design Principal: Pipih Priyatna **Design Team:** Desti Ayu, Megan Agung **Landscape:** Pipih Priyatna Architects & Contractors Office
Contractor: Pipih Priyatna Contractors **Structure:** Hermanto Subagijo, HERSUB

JS House

Tulodong, South Jakarta
Studio TonTon

JS House is located in a private residential area near Jakarta's primary business district. Consequently, soaring high-rise buildings and busy roads surround the homes in the area. Studio TonTon took advantage of this condition by designing a house that stands out amidst the formidable skyscrapers in its background.

Even at first glance, the house exhibits an intriguing focal point with its sharp upper mass extruding out toward the street. This bold impression is further emphasized by a predominantly bare-concrete finish, which envelops the building. Another notable focal point is the vertical garden, which overgrows the rest of the façade, adding shade and a surge of greenery to balance the monochromatic exterior.

Left: Creeper plants cover the façade, providing the glass openings with shade.

Top: The topmost floor of the house functions as a rooftop garden and viewing deck. **Bottom:** Large glass windows allow an intimate relation between indoor and outdoor space. **Opposite top:** The house bears a distinctive façade with an angular protruding mass and plant-covered wall.

The home's interior is just as striking as its exterior. Conforming to the client's requirement for a dynamic space plan, the building's axis rotates against the site's orientation. This design approach made it possible to create irregular spaces both inside and out. The relation between the two spaces is kept intimate by glass walls, which blur the boundary between exterior and interior. Because the site is located near a busy road, the house is oriented inwards and encircled by vertical garden walls. This configuration maintains a sense of privacy for occupants.

Consisting of four levels, the house exhibits a different function on each level. A wine cellar and service area are located on the basement level. The ground level has been designed as an open and light communal family area alongside a garden.

Bedrooms located on the upper level have wide glass openings, which allow occupants to enjoy the greenery of the vertical garden. At the highest level, an observation deck covered with grass and equipped with white furniture boasts a 360-degree urban view.

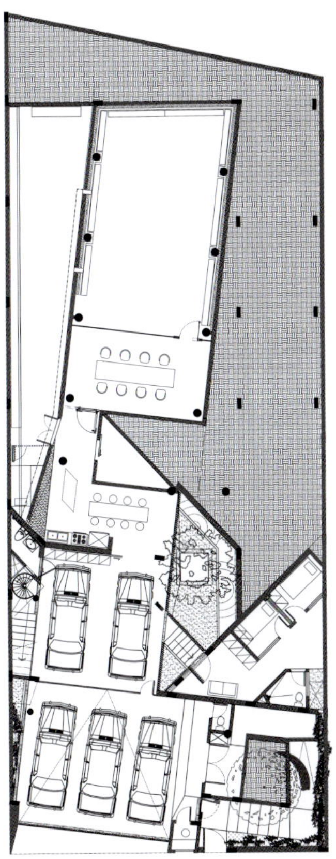

Basement floor plan

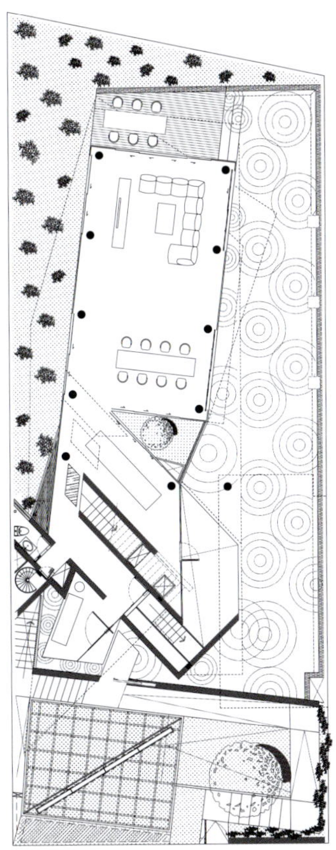

Ground-floor plan

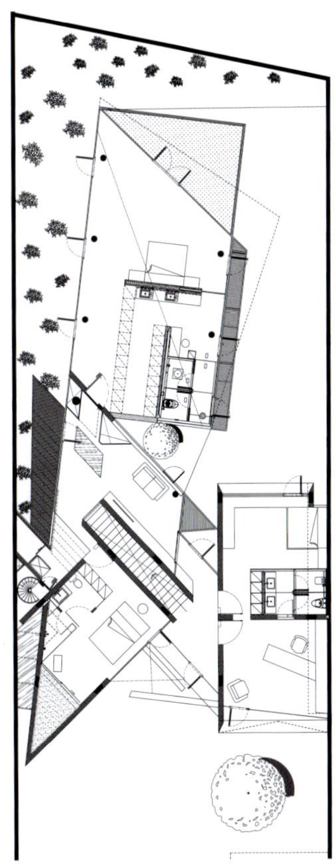

First-floor plan

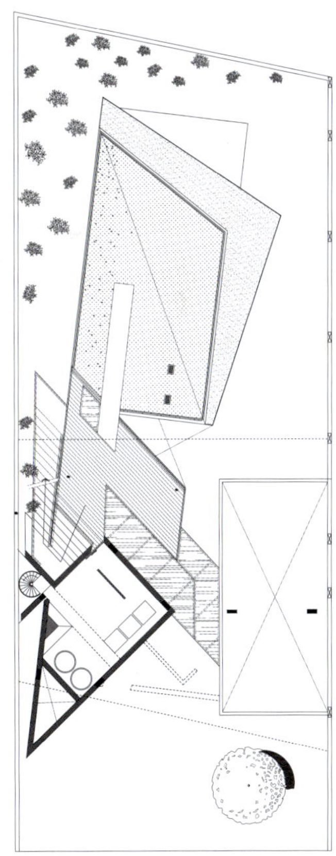

Second-floor plan 0 4m

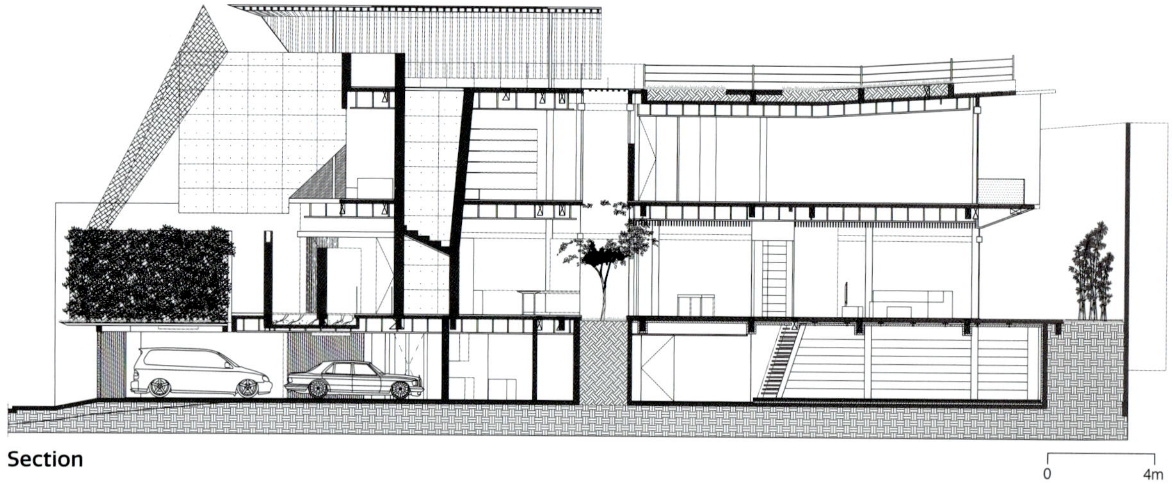

Section

Site Area: 6975 ft² (648 m²) **Floor Area:** 10,333 ft² (960 m²) **Photographer:** Sonny Sandjaya **Design Period:** 2011–2012 **Construction Period:** 2012–2015 **Design Principal:** Antonio Liu, Ferry Ridwan **Design Team:** Gita Mustika Sumitra, Ivan Susanto, Kezia Paramita **Interior:** Studio TonTon **Landscape:** PT Hujan Mas **Contractor:** PT Dwitunggal Mandirijaya **Structure:** Hadi & Associates **M&E:** PT Dwitunggal Mandirijaya **Lighting:** Studio TonTon

The home's materials have been kept simple without additional finishes. This creates a beautiful combination of various textures. The interior walls are dominated by exposed concrete complete with form holes, which accentuate the residence's character. The natural light from the large windows and shifted skylights helps emphasize the textural detail of the overall heavy material, much like spotlights inside a gallery. Wooden flooring has been used to balance the home's rugged feel and adds a warm ambience throughout the interior space.

The outdoor area showcases a series of appealing spatial experiences. To reach the house, people must go through a narrow ramp from the front entrance. The distinctive sides of the ramp—concrete wall on one side and vertical garden on the other—impart different sensations as people walk through. A reflecting pond placed at the entrance produces soothing water sounds and filters noise from the front road. The surrounding landscape design allows residents to experience the beauty of nature despite the metropolitan context. The combination of water, wood, and exposed concrete enriches the home with natural nuances.

Studio TonTon have designed much more than a dwelling. JS House enriches the senses through a motley assortment of materials and lively spatial experiences.

Opposite bottom: The living area is flanked by a vertical garden on the left side and swimming pool on the right. **Top:** The rotated axis produces sharp corners within the house, giving the space a dynamic impression. **Bottom:** The second floor enjoys a lush view of the vertical garden.

Light + Light House

Jati Padang, South Jakarta

Studio TonTon

The notion of fusing a building with nature was at the core of the design for this home located in an exclusive housing complex in Jakarta. There were two main aims applied to the design. The first was to bring as much natural light and airflow into the building as possible. The Second was to create a building that appeared to be lightweight in order to prevent it from dominating the surrounding natural environment. In response to these design approaches, the project is named Light + Light House.

The concept of merging nature is immediately evident upon stepping through main entrance located on the side of the building. Natural elements of water, timber, and stone surround the semi-outdoor corridor leading to the main entrance. The door is directly connected to the main circulation route that crosses over at the heart of the building, separating the building mass into four sections.

Along this cross axis, the architects placed a void and applied a skylight system, allowing sunlight to freely enter the building. Wood panels along the skylight regulate excessive sun heat. In addition, the architects also designed a pond along the void. The presence of water inside the house complements the vision of the building uniting with the nature. The pond has been installed within the airflow route, bringing a fresh and soothing ambience into the building.

Left: The lush hanging garden covers half of the house's façade.

1 Study room
2 Living room
3 Dining room
4 Master bedroom
5 Master bathroom

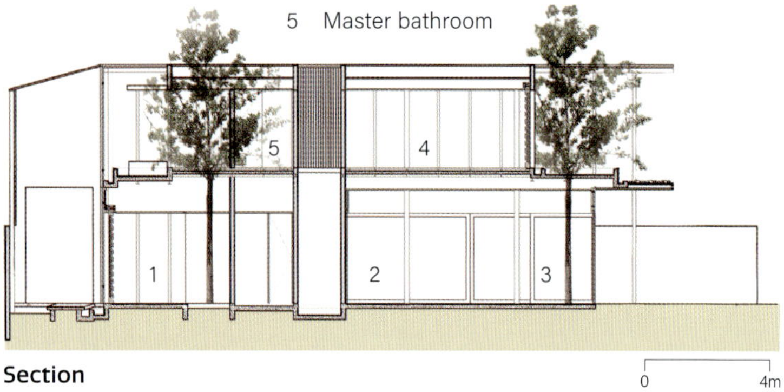

Section

To support the building, the architects utilized steel structures as the main architectural morphology. In an effort to achieve the desired lightweight appearance, most of the steel columns and blocks at the front of the house have been incorporated with glass. The formed building mass at the front holds a guest bedroom and a living room on the ground floor, and a master bedroom on the upper floor. In contrast to the steel and glass appearance at the front, exposed concrete has been used at the rear of the building. The rear houses a dining room, kitchen, and a service area on the ground floor, as well as a bathroom and a workstation on the upper floor. The home's geometric lines will eventually become concealed behind lush vines growing from the roof, further accentuating the vision for a home united with nature.

Opposite bottom left: Hidden within the thick vertical garden is the main door of the house. **Opposite top right:** Despite being inside the house, the use of rough materials and natural elements give the sensation of being outside. **Top:** Tree branches protrude the floor, bringing nature into the bathroom. **Bottom:** Maintaining the existing trees on the site and incorporating them into the design is one of the ways the architects ensured the longevity of the greenery despite the existence of the building.

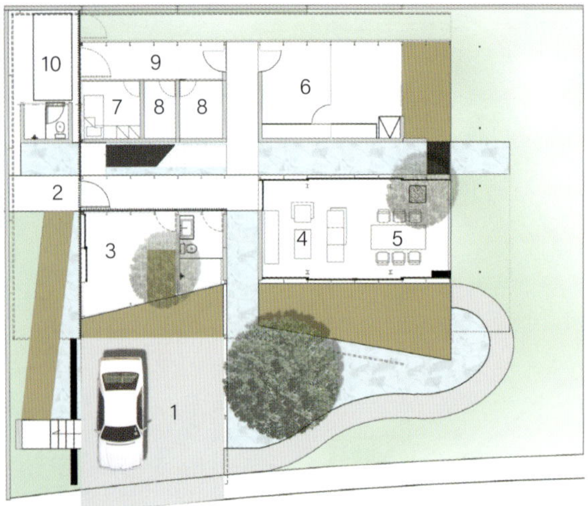

Ground-floor plan

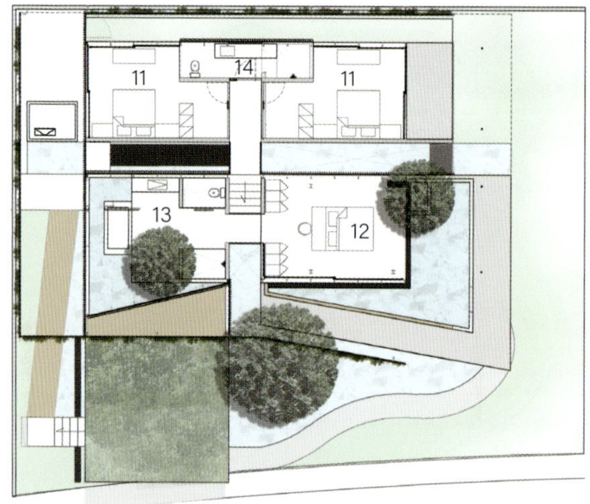

First-floor plan

0 4m

1 Carport
2 Entrance
3 Study room
4 Living room
5 Dining room
6 Kitchen
7 Maid's room
8 Storage
9 Linen room
10 Drying area
11 Bedroom
12 Master bedroom
13 Master bathroom
14 Bathroom

The architects' execution of a design that appreciates the surrounding nature has given the home a balanced feel. The combination of stone, timber, water, greenery, and a play of light and shadow, has achieved a tranquil freshness indoors. The design approach to air circulation—the void and skylight at the heart of the building—make the home seem larger than it actually is. These are only some of the reasons why the owner—a renowned Indonesian art director—is proud to live in a Studio TonTon-designed home.

Left & right: The dining room is connected with the terrace, extending the space toward the outdoor. **Opposite:** The night view from the spacious backyard of the house.

Site Area: 5059+ ft² (470+ m²) **Floor Area:** 3875+ ft² (360+ m²) **Photographer:** Sonny Sandjaya, Sjahrial Iqbal, Mario Wibowo **Design Period:** 2007–2010 **Construction Period:** 2010–2012 **Design Principal:** Antony Liu, Ferry Ridwan **Design Team:** Ivan Susanto, Azhar Efendi **Interior:** Studio TonTon **Landscape:** Puri Gajah Nursery and Landscape **Contractor:** PT Griya Kreasi **Structure:** PT Hersub Konsultan Struktur **M&E:** PT Makesthi Enggal Engineering **Lighting:** Studio TonTon

Lounge Villa

Lembang, West Java

Han Awal & Partners Architects

Lounge Villa is nestled on a slope that faces the hillside of Dago in Bandung. The slope's highest point is level with the road of the residential complex in which it is located. Lush, free-growing vegetation disguises the house from the road.

Aside from the veiling vegetation, the home is also disguised by the site's contours, which consist of a steep descending valley. From the road, this gives the impression that the house is single-story.

The architect responded to the site's contours by minimizing the contiguity between the building and the ground. Based on this idea, the construction of the building followed a pile structure design, with the application of thin, continuous concrete columns to support its four stories.

The pile structure created an empty space beneath the house, which resulted in minimum contact with the ground and a reduced structural footprint.

Nevertheless, in anticipation of potential landslides, the architect insisted on applying soil reinforcing measures, such as the construction of walls made from stacks of river stone. A bridge was also implemented into the design to prevent the building from leaning toward the sloping site. The bridge also functions as a carport, which hangs over the sloping terrain and offers occupants a thrilling experience when they cross it.

Left: The design utilizies the steep landscape, providing occupants with striking views of natural panoramas.

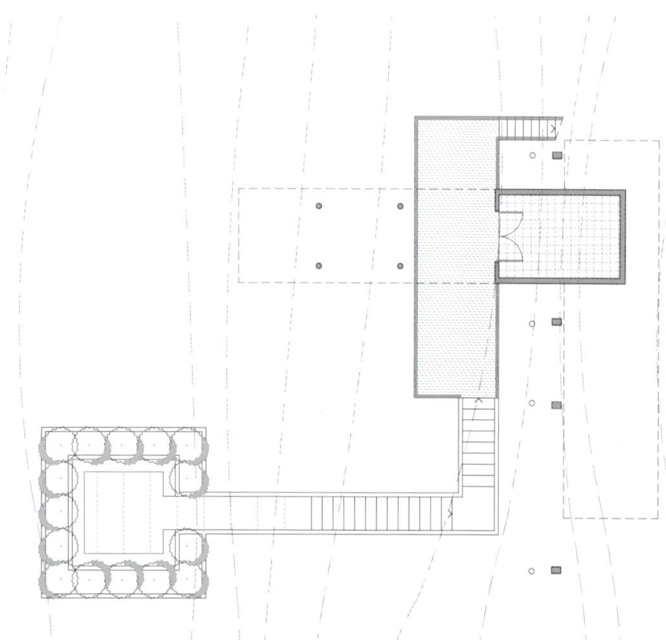

Basement floor plan

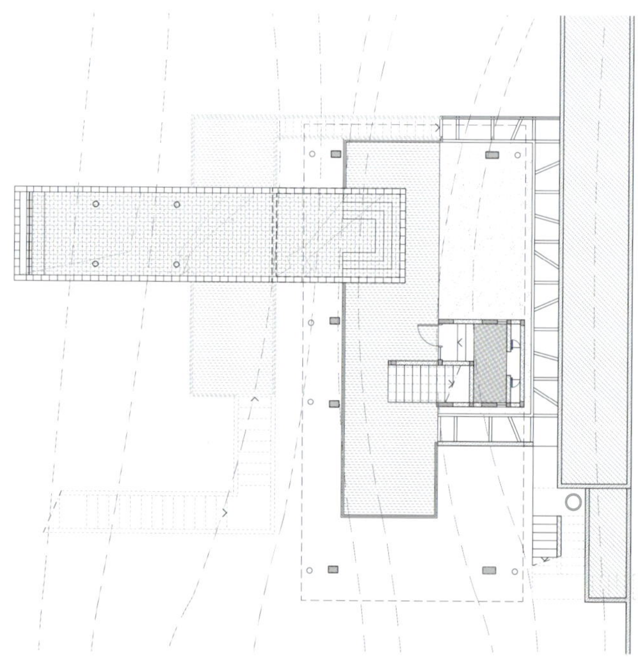

Ground-floor plan

Lounge Villa

A spacious terrace invites occupants to enjoy the scenery before accessing the house through the fourth floor. The fourth floor—the highest floor—acts as the transition area to the center of the house, which is located on the third floor and below. The living room, kitchen, and pantry are located on the ground floor, while the bedrooms are situated on the basement level. In contrast with the bordered spaces on the upper floors, the architect filled the lower-basement level with open spaces. On this lowest floor, a terrace faces toward the site's backside, which consists of a descending hillside graced with a scenic view.

Opposite top: Wide openings in the living room help minimize the use of artificial lighting during the day. **Left:** The view over the distant paddy fields is an exquisite backdrop to the dining area. **Right:** The occupants can enjoy the soothing scenery from almost every bedroom in the house.

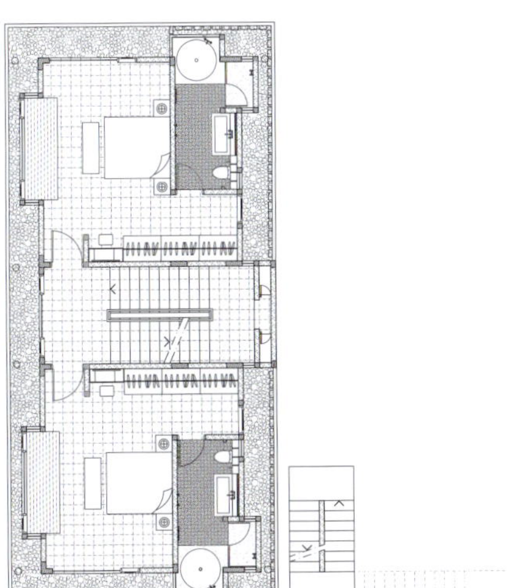

First-floor plan

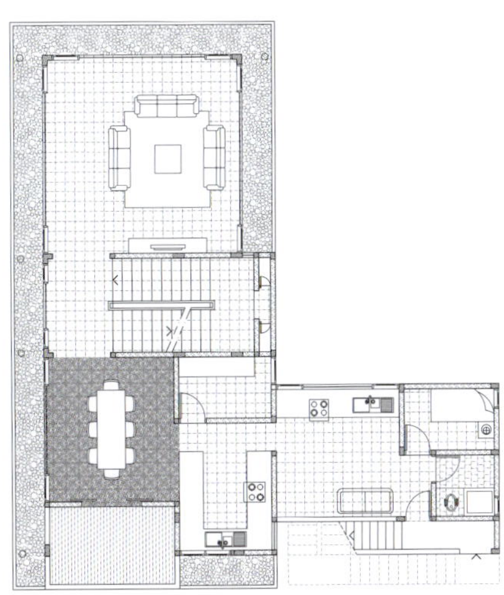

Second-floor plan

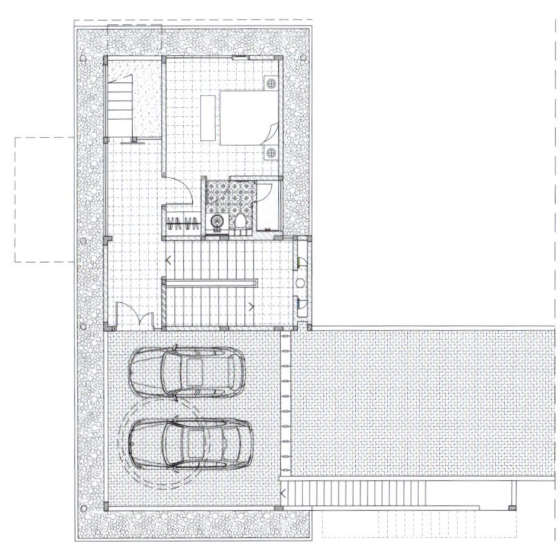

Third-floor plan

Site Area: 12,971 ft² (1205 m²) **Floor Area:** 6157 ft² (572 m²) **Photographer:** Sonny Sandjaya **Design Period:** 2008–2011 **Design Principal:** Yori Antar **Design Team:** Ricardo Dwiputra **Interior:** delighting **Landscape:** Intaran Design **Contractor:** PT Parama Dharma **Structure:** Muchamad Umar **M&E:** Doddy Ruurdoto **Lighting:** SSA Lighting Solution

Lounge Villa

Located next to the terrace is a pool designed to hang over the hill, and an outdoor lounge, which leans toward the descending hill. List planks on the home's exterior indicate the clear separation of floors, while thin and continuous columns give the home a lightweight appearance.

Although the color white dominates the homes presence, natural materials such as the wood used on the window frames, doors, and terrace floors as well as the brick structure that shapes perforated walls on the second floor, give the home a warm and balanced feel.

The use of open space in the home's design aims to utilize the site's scenic potential and give occupants the opportunity to become completely immersed in the natural surrounds.

Opposite: Light-colored walls and natural tones from wood and brick materials are set against green surroundings. **Top:** The terrace offers privacy as it is situated on the ground floor and shielded with stone walls. **Bottom:** The infinity pool on the ground floor boasts views of the hills and rice fields.

Manhattan Villa

Canggu, Bali
US&P Architects

Villa Manhattan is a private retreat located in Canggu, Bali. From paddy fields to black-sand beaches, the surrounding landscape is beautifully diverse. The villa's modern geometrical shape stands distinctly among the verdant paddy fields. The client desired a complete getaway that would capture quality views and complement the beauty of the landscape.

The house is inspired by Bali's open tropical spaces, particularly the paddy fields. It has been built on a terrace structure to respond the site. Inside, the terrace structure has been translated into a split-level plan. Distinct living areas are separated into five levels to suit a variety of activities. Each level is connected by flights of stairs. This creates a continuous flow and a spacious multi-dimensional feel throughout the home, while still providing cosy, discreet spaces for a variety of activities. This design also allows varying atmospheric experiences under one roof and enables occupants the option of socializing without constraints.

Left: The home's staggered form that follows the site's contour gives it a unique identity.

Bottom left: Frameless glass doors have been used to break down barriers and create a continuous vista from the exterior to the interior. **Bottom right:** The split-level plan allows for fluid circulation through all five layers of the house. **Opposite top:** The house enjoys lush greenery as a surrounding panorama.

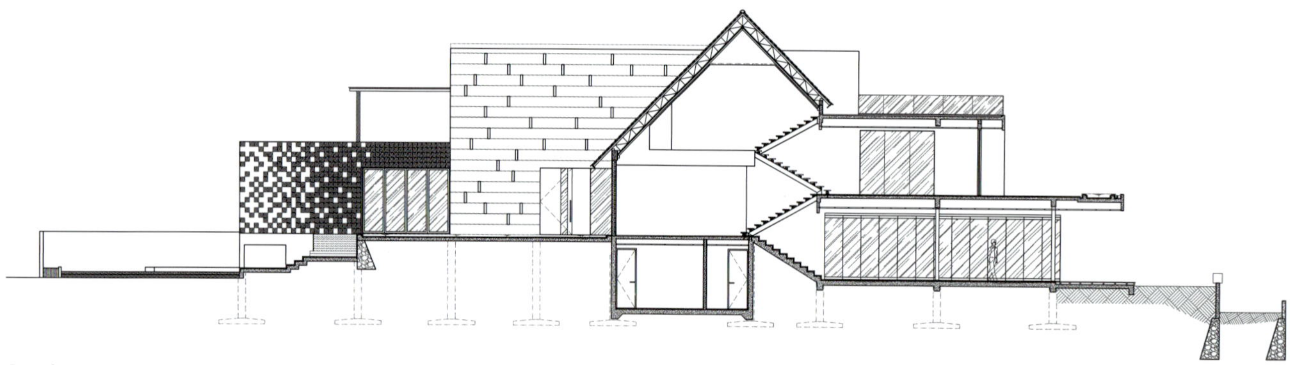

Section

The house exudes a Balinese resort-style ambience and is characterized by the interplay of material flowing from interior to exterior spaces. The detail of craftsmanship from local artists and local materials evident in the home's finishes further enhance its eclectic resort-like feel. Wooden walls and floors inside the bedroom give the space a warm and earthy feel. Backed up against a padded wall, the four-poster bed adds a sense of elegance, sophistication, and exclusivity to the bedroom. Neutral bedding and cool-colored pillows have been used to prevent the space from feeling oppressive. Clean lines and uncluttered surfaces in combination with warm materials, rich textures, and soothing colors result in a cosy haven for relaxation. Travertine, a luxurious material that accentuates modernity, has been used for the walls in other areas of the house. Wood has also been used for a deck that flows from the living room to the swimming pool. The house showcases a harmonious balance between the clean, contemporary lines of the architecture and the calming tones and textures of the internal and external finishes, all of which are complemented by exterior hardscape and softscape designs.

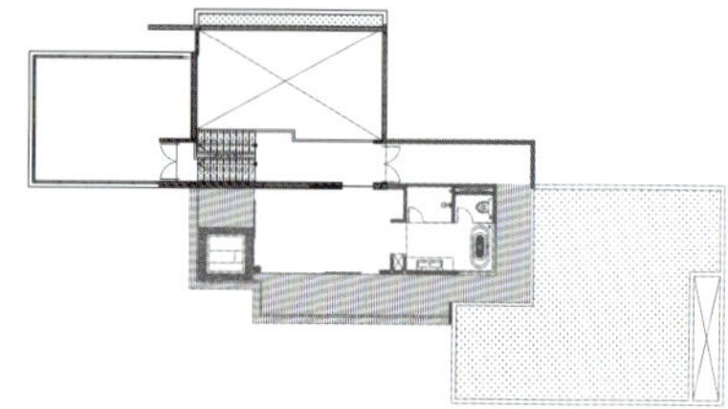

Roof floor plan

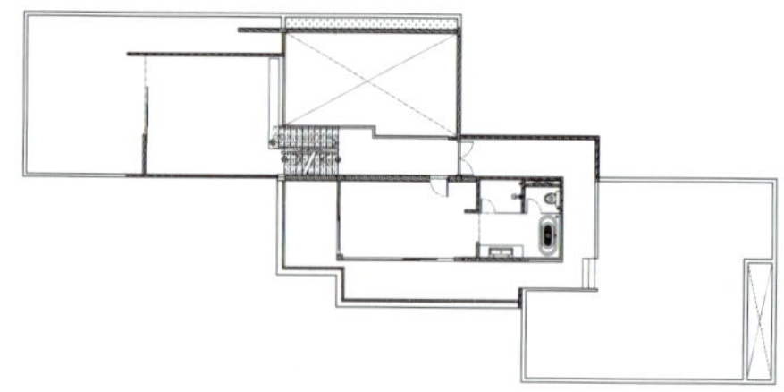

Upper floor plan

Not unlike the interior, the home's exterior spaces have also been designed to be functional. For example, the concrete deck on the rooftop level serves as both an outdoor communal area and private spa. In order to make full use of all space available, the home's design intentionally blurs the boundaries between interior and exterior. The rooms are separated yet connected by frameless glass doors, which allow uninterrupted views toward open areas.

The architect wanted to create an entrance procession that was rich in natural visual elements, from the basement up to the viewing deck. Upon entering from the side entrance at the basement, occupants must walk through a long corridor adorned with a skylight from the above pond. This creates a dramatic lighting effect. In contrast, the entrance from the front of the house is a more open space, accompanied by the trickling sound of water from a reflection pond.

US&P Architects have combined the beautiful scenery of Canggu with modern architecture to create a harmonious living environment.

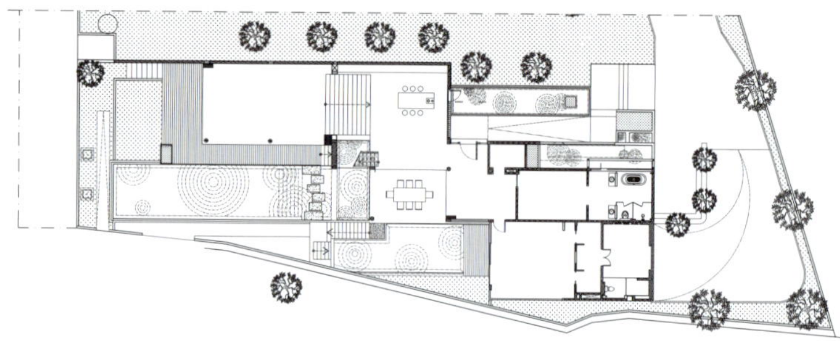

Ground-floor plan

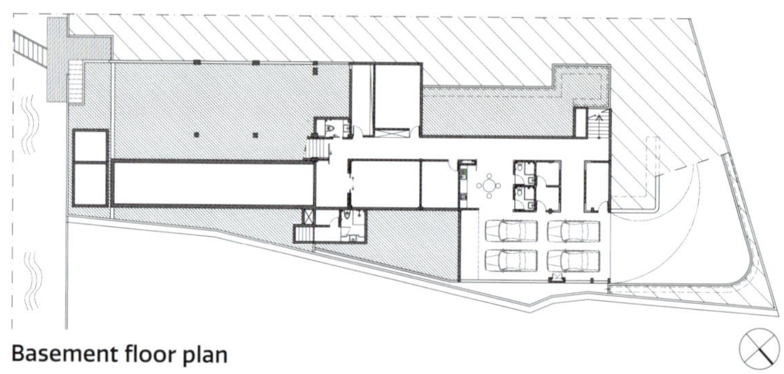

Basement floor plan

Top left: The house incorporates plenty of outdoor space for residents to enjoy nature. **Bottom right:** Striking artwork and various wall textures are incorporated in the interior, enlivening and enriching the character of the space. **Opposite:** The split-level plan allows for fluid circulation through all five layers of the house.

Site Area: 7858 ft² (730 m²) **Floor Area:** 7610 ft² (707 m²) **Photographer:** Fernando Gomulya **Design Period:** 2011–2014 **Construction Period:** 2013–2014
Design Principal: Her Pramtama, Timmy Anggara Arthawardhana **Design Team:** Reza Kaedy **Interior:** YAHP Studio
Landscape: US&P Architects **Contractor:** Umah Bali **Structure:** Agus Surjadi **M&E:** Umah Bali

Merapi Hill House

Special Region of Yogyakarta
Dwi Kurniawan

The northern part of the Special Region of Yogyakarta is home to several active volcanos, including Mount Merapi, which is heavily contoured with slopes and steep valleys.

This project is located at the foot of Mount Merapi, on a flat area at the top of a valley with a river flowing roughly 66 feet (20 meters) below. Due to heavy volcanic activity, the area is prone to earthquakes. In response to this, the architect designed a ground retaining wall on one side of the cliff, followed by terraces. This built landscape was designed to enhance views around the site. Despite this man-made landscape, the architect was determined to not cut down any existing trees inside the plot. This is evident in at the home's entrance, which is abundant with meandering greenery.

A primary consideration in the design of the home's layout was the incredibly beautiful view surrounding the plot. The bedrooms and the living room were designed to capture views of the untouched valleys across the river. A small sky pool was also built at the back of the house to capture additional valley views.

Left: Existing vegetation literally touches and merges with the sky pool hanging over the cliff.

Opposite & top: The house is built with low walls and deliberately exposes the rafters of the ceiling. **Right:** The veranda is one of the best spots to enjoy the soothing verdant panorama surrounding the house.

The architect focused largely on creating an ambient interior. An exposed traditional wooden roof and wooden furniture impart a serene atmosphere within the home. The walls, which are deliberately built at three-quarter height, give the space a large and open feel.

Although the house is located in an earthquake-prone area, it managed to withstand any structural damage when Yogyakarta was hit in 2006. Nevertheless, the architect still endeavored to anticipate such risks and in addition to the retaining wall, the sky pool also acts as a retaining structure. Extending up to 56 feet (17 meters), the pool's large support columns reach down and grasp the lower ground surface. As a result, Merapi Hill House is a dwelling that wisely responds to its dramatic context by incorporating necessary design precautions while accentuating the plot's grand panorama.

Top left: The meandering entranceway is the result of the architect's determination to retain existing trees. **Top right:** Stones taken from the river adjacent to the plot have been used in the wall of the entranceway. **Bottom:** The architect's treatment of the plot allows the house to merge with the surrounding natural beauty. **Opposite:** The house is nestled among undulating hills at the foot of Mount Merapi and surrounded by an array of wild vegetation.

Site Area: 75,347+ ft² (7000+ m²) **Floor Area:** 4306+ ft² (400+ m²) **Photographer:** Sonny Sandjaya

batur 9

The Monolithic House

Semarang, Central Java
MSSM Associates

The design of a house as a reflection of an owner's personality is often applied in one of two ways: the bold, extroverted, and extravagant; and the reserved, refined, and minimalistic. In the case of The Monolithic House, the latter applies. Located at the higher part of a contoured neighborhood, the house conceals a hidden treasure—a vista facing the hilltops of southwest Semarang.

To translate the needs and character of the owner, the architect proposed a simple configuration. The box-shaped mass is formed by nine rectangular grids on each floor, with the living and dining in the midmost grid as the center of the house. Surrounding the central grid are private and service areas, such as bedrooms, the kitchen, and garage. However, unrestrained by the grid system, the home's façade represents modern style, if not brutalist architecture to emphasize secrecy through minimal openings and a blatant concrete finish. This titular Monolithic style completely represents the front expression of the house.

Left: The rigid exterior with minimal openings and unfinished concrete to maximize privacy.

Contrary to the restrictive front façade, the interior of the house exhibits a fluid connection of spaces. Inside the dark steel archway entrance, a two-story foyer offers a distinct experience of spaciousness. In the living area, however, a low-ceiling height and wooden envelope arouse intimacy before reaching the dining area that, again, expands as a void up to the second floor. The transition from the reclusiveness of the home's façade culminates as the openness of the dining space extends toward the fully transparent glass doors. Without any privacy concerns, the translucent partition seamlessly stretches from the dining area to the bedroom, while a continuous wooden terrace connects both rooms and serves as a transition to a private garden, providing expansive views over the lush hilltops.

Careful positioning of skylights throughout the house further enhances the interior's dynamic sequence. The vertical source of light creates playful geometric shadows on the perpendicular surfaces below. Notably, an extruding art installation, which adds additional and interesting layers of shadow, is embedded below one of the skylights adjacent to the living area. Similar to how the skylights embody the home, artworks also adorn the interior as well as contrasting or complementing colored furniture, defining the whole interior as a flowing work of art.

Top left: Playful shadows from the skylight create defined geometric shapes on the surface of the wall. **Right:** As the extension of the living space, the dining area expresses spaciousness that expands toward the transparent glass doors.

Despite the contrast between the home's exterior and interior, precise geometric forms conveying modern architecture consistently feature in both. It is this constant precision—thanks to flawless construction details—that harmoniously unifies the home's overall design.

To passers-by, the home's rigid exterior make it seem like a fortress, frigid and lacking a sense of home. But for the owner, this unfinished concrete confine is a treasured shelter that repels outsider attention and allows its inhabitants to enjoy a haven, all for themselves. The home's secluded design embraces nature as a context integral to the experience of living within. Through its meticulous composition, Monolithic House is a fine example of how the architect has captured a perfect balance between the beauty of nature and the comfort of a house, all within a modern interpretation.

Top: The continuous wood finish creates an intimate scale within the living space. **Opposite:** The wooden deck makes a subtle transition from the interior to the private garden with expansive view of Semarang hilltops.

Site Area: 9688 ft^2 (900 m^2) **Floor Area:** 8611 ft^2 (800 m^2) **Photographer:** Sonny Sandjaya **Design Period:** 2012
Design Principal: Revano Satria **Interior:** RSI Group **Landscape:** Jamadi
Contractor: Lukito **Structure:** Lukito **M&E:** RSI Group **Lighting:** RSI Group

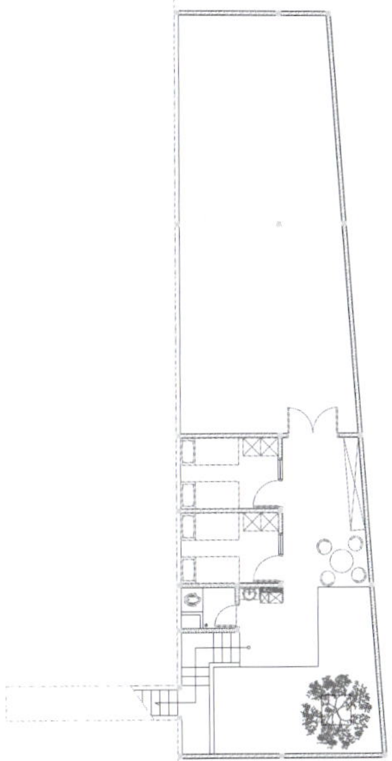

Basement floor plan

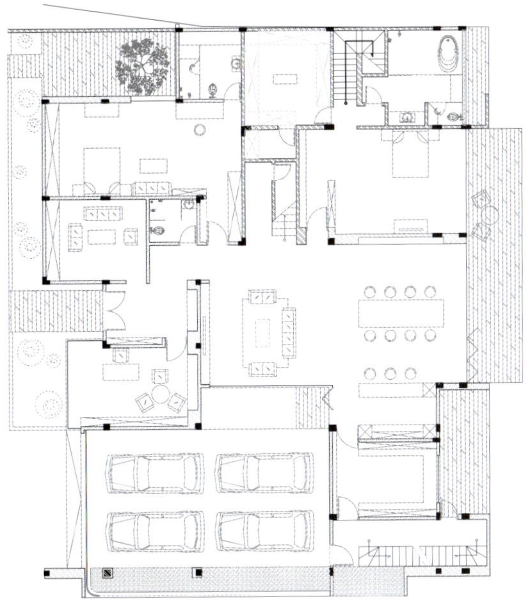

Ground-floor plan

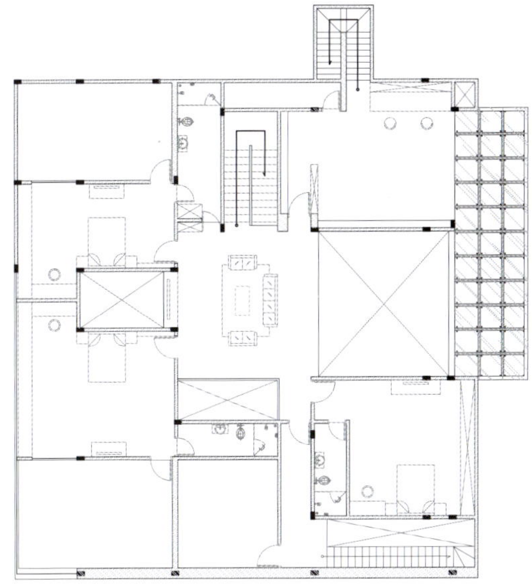

First-floor plan

The Mori

Bandung, West Java
LABO.

Despite its location on the outskirts of Bandung's city center, the LABO. *thermori* site—*mori* meaning forest in Japanese—is populated by a cluster of mahogany trees. A 52.5-foot (16-meter) height difference between the site's highest and lowest point enhance its dramatic appeal. The top of the slope enjoys an expansive view toward the relatively untouched terrain of Bandung's northern area—a surging carpet of greenery dotted with residences.

There are various approaches architects can take when designing dwellings located in dense vegetation. In this project, LABO. proffer respect for the land by taking up just enough area for the buildings and cherishing nature as part of the living space.

The Mori refers to the 14,068 square feet (1307 square meters) of land owned by couple Nelly L. Daniel and Deddy Wahjudi, both architects and the founders of the Bandung-based firm LABO. Upon this land, LABO. has established their architectural office and family home along with three additional dwelling units. A stepped amphitheatre cuts down the slope of the site for easy navigation. It also creates a space for gathering. LABO. plan for the land to eventually hold a total of six dwelling units, all bridged by a connecting walkway, which also functions as a viewing gallery.

Left: Wide windows look out from LABO.'s office to the row of mahogany trees ahead.

Left: The dwelling units have been designed as a hybrid of massive walls and wide openings overlooking the best views. **Opposite top:** Creeper plants on the windows and ceilings shroud the living and dining areas. **Opposite bottom:** Mahogany trees frame the view toward the hill regions of Bandung. Located further down the slope are other dwellings in the complex.

Positioned atop the slope is the office: a single-story building oriented parallel to the best view. Wide glass doors on one side of the building look out toward the row of mahogany trees and green hills beyond. The other side of the wall has been doubled with wire mesh for creeper plants to grow upon. LABO. thoroughly welcomes the presence of nature inside their workspace. The roof as and indoor ceiling are covered with enveloping creeper plants intended to soften the sound of heavy rainfall and refresh the occupants' experience. The indoor space enjoys natural ventilation with fresh air moving freely between the open glass doors and space beneath the roof.

Across from the office is Nelly and Deddy's personal home. It was the first dwelling unit to be built on the site, hence the name Rumah#1. The residence sits lightly upon the land and has a footprint of 15 by 25 feet (4.5 by 7.5 meters). Having lived in Japan for over five years, Nelly and Deddy are very familiar with the principles of compact design. The limited availability of land in Japan's metropolitan areas meant that living spaces had to be efficient and utilize every inch of available space.

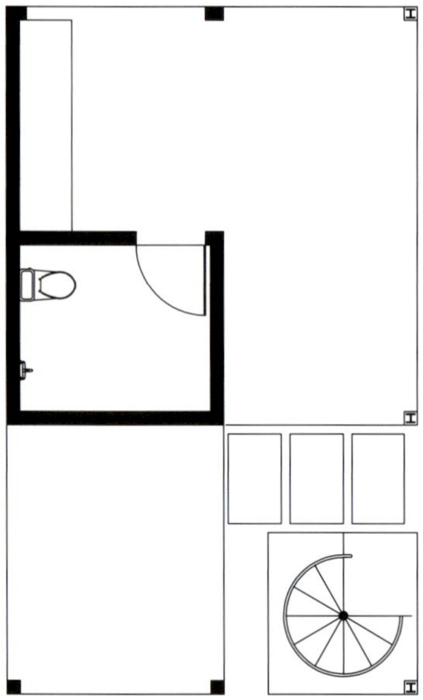

Ground-floor plan

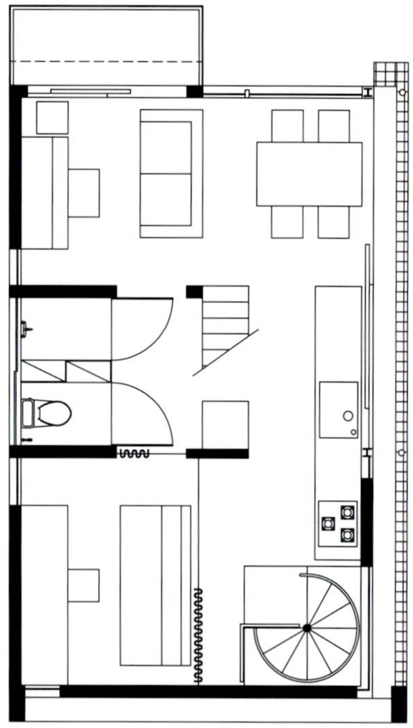

First-floor plan

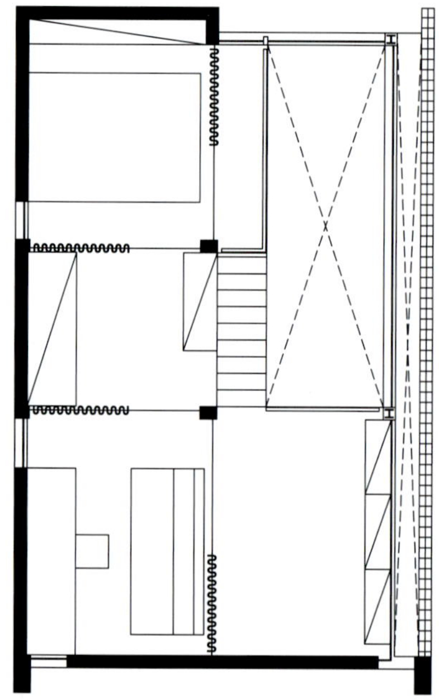

Mezzanine floor plan

0 2m

These principles of efficiency and an emphasis on nature informed the design concept of The Mori dwellings. Spaces were designed to take up as little area as possible. The ground level of Rumah#1 takes the form of an open and shaded area without walls, and houses the pantry as an extension of the office. On one corner, a spiral staircase ascends toward the second level where the main living space is located. Shrouded with creeper plants from floor to roof, the kitchen and dining area function as the heart of daily family activities.

From the living space, a narrow staircase leads up bedrooms on a mezzanine level. The rooms are fluidly partitioned by curtains, which are analogous to Japanese paper screens. Contrary to the glass openings of the living area, these sleeping quarters face concrete walls for privacy.

By balancing spatial necessity with an appreciation for nature, LABO. has created individual dwellings of hybrid expression and function, all of which encapsulate the context of the surrounding forest.

Left: In order to replicate the efficiency of apartment living, spaces are fluidly interconnected, with the main bedroom overlooking the dining area. **Opposite:** A staircase made out of a metal plate connects the second level to the mezzanine floor above.

Site Area: 14,068 ft² (1307 m²) **Gross Floor Area:** 5005 ft² (465 m²) **Photographer:** Sonny Sandjaya **Design Period:** 2008–2015 **Construction Period:** 2008–2016 **Design Principal:** Deddy Wahjudi, Nelly L. Daniel **Design Team:** Hamal O. Pangestu, Angga Rosiawan, Mariska Pratimi, Gilang Arenza, Abdillah Aji, Galih Priyambodo, Ivan Danny, Aron Baranuri **Interior:** LABO. **Landscape:** Greenbaum Indonesia **Contractor:** LABO. **Structure:** LABO. **M&E:** LABO. **Lighting:** LABO.

MW House

Semarang, Central Java
andramatin

Architecture is a product of the negotiation process between the clients' needs, the architects' style, and the condition of the surroundings. If clients have only a few specific requests the architect is granted a certain freedom of expression, which can be advantageous to a design. This happened to be the case with MW House and it compelled architect andramatin to revert back to the purest form of geometry, the box, which can be transformed to achieve impressive spatial experiences.

From the outside, MW House appears as three boxy masses: a vertical box stands beside two horizontally stacked boxes. This gives the home a rigid appearance. The gray, patterned façade of the vertical-standing box enhances the contrast between the masses, creating an attractive accent. Built on an elevation, the whole entity of the house welcomes occupants via a steep landscape and through a garage door. This single entrance and steep landscape acts as a barrier of sorts from the outside world and gives the home a superior quality.

The home's east-to-west orientation allows the upper box to receive plenty of direct sunshine throughout the day. In order to create air circulation, the architect suggested a layering of the window on the front part of the upper box, which is the owner's bedroom. An opening at the bottom of this layer provides the owner with a view of the outdoors and allows sunshine to enter the room. This upper box is shifted from the home's axis, forming a cantilever at the south to shade the terrace below. This form allows the terrace to be used in any kind of weather.

Left: The extreme cantilever combined with the window camouflage enhances the home's appearance.

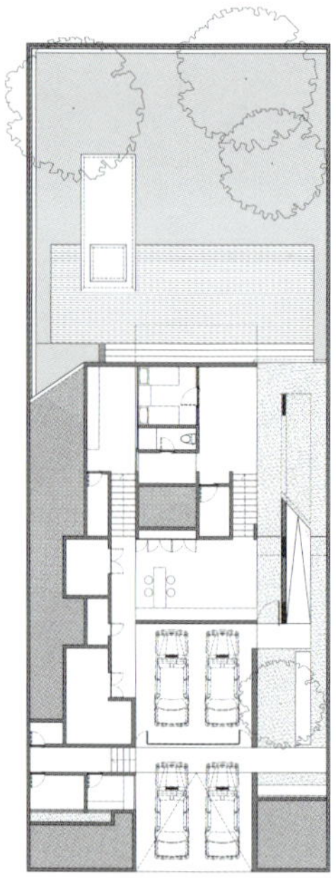

Ground-floor plan

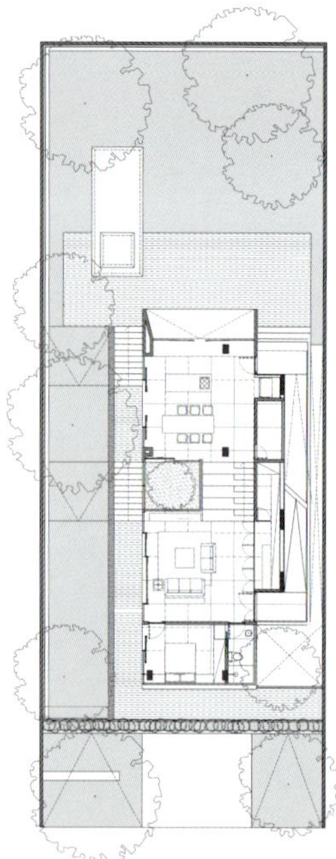

First-floor plan

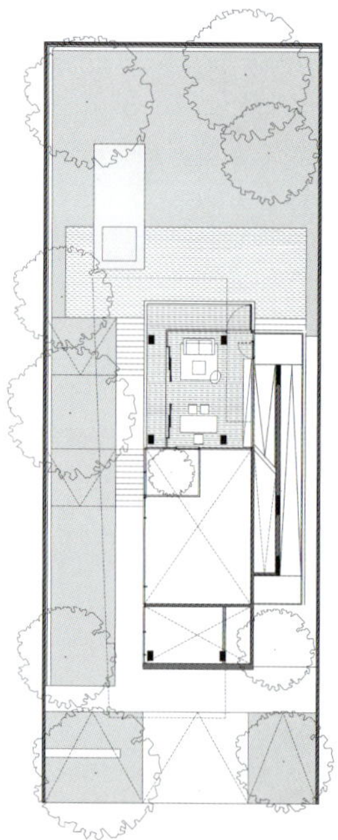

Mezzanine floor plan

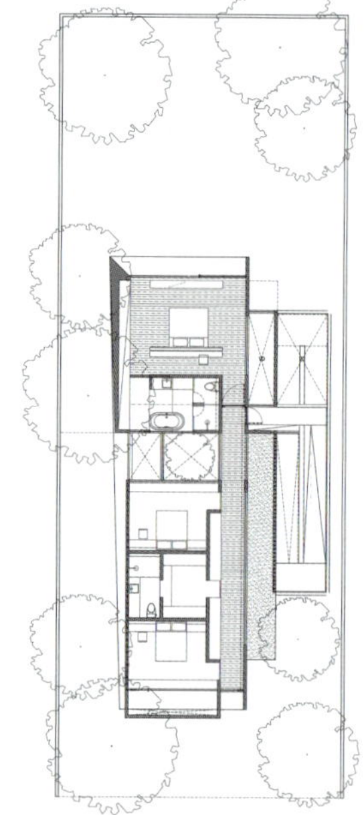

Second-floor plan

0 6m

The home's lower box comprises communal spaces for the family. The interior of the mass was designed with a split-level method, which consists of three different levels. This means that the living room, dining room, and the workroom are each connected by stairs, creating a continuous flow throughout the home and enabling interactions between occupants. A light well containing a mini garden acts as a unique boundary space within the dining room. The well also allows sunlight to enter the home and brings nature indoors.

The vertical mass on the home's north side functions as a vertical circulation space. A ramp located alongside the mass has been used as a transitional element to create a continuous spatial experience, which is translated into other areas of the home. Its packed porous stones smoothly circulate air and fulfill the clients' wish for a space that can work efficiently without air conditioning. Varying patterns of light and shadow filter through the porous stone, creating a cinematic experience.

Left: Other than dramatizing the cantilever, the gap between masses maintains the pure geometry of a box that forms the house. **Opposite top left:** A porous façade covers the ramp, giving a unique lighting effect to the space. **Opposite top right:** Each space has a large opening that connects to the outdoor area, unifying the garden and interior. **Opposite bottom:** A spacious dining area occupies the same space as the kitchen and has access to the light well and outdoor area.

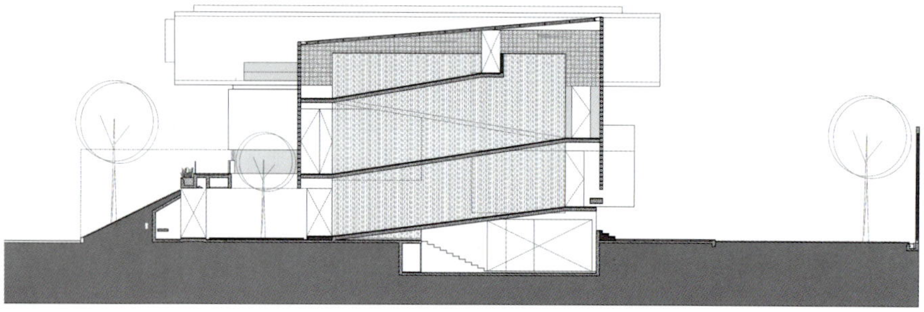

Section

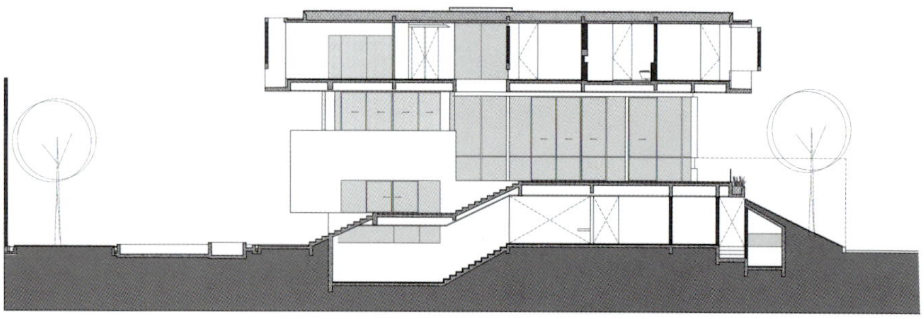

Section

Other capturing elements of the home include the floating cantilever of the upper box and the structural columns in the center of the mass, which have intentionally been left exposed, creating a gap between the upper and lower mass. This bold design feature further enhances the home's dramatic appeal and allowed the architect maximum possibility in terms of how the boxes could be composed. MW House demonstrates sumptuous spatial experiences through clever applications of a modest geometric form.

Bottom left: The ramp is hidden from the rest of the house in a secluded space. **Bottom right:** The top floor walkway allows residents to see the porous mass and light well on both sides. **Opposite:** The wall openings in the back elevation give hints of lights at night, creating a sense of drama.

Site Area: 4424 ft² (411 m²) **Floor Area:** 3003 ft² (279 m²) **Photographer:** Sonny Sandjaya **Design Period:** 2000–2001 **Construction Period:** 2013–2015 **Design Principal:** Andra Matin **Design Team:** Ady Putra Sanjaya, Suhaedi **Contractor:** Alex Gandung **Structure:** Hadi Jahja **M&E:** Eranto, Mega Wahono **Lighting:** andramatin

Pavilion 26 Golf Residence

Tangerang, Banten

Stanley Wangsadihardja, Susy Gunawan

The owners of Pavilion 26 required additional space to accommodate a growing family, host social activities, and house their art collection. In response, Stanley Wangsadihardja and Susy Gunawan constructed a supporting pavilion to complement the function of their existing house.

In a book titled *Glass House,* Nicky Adams said, "As life in the 21st century becomes less formalized, and the importance of being relaxed in the home environment grows, houses are called upon to evolve to suit these ever changing needs." This is how an architect responds to the evolving needs of a family. As a supporting building, the architectural programming of Pavilion 26 is less complicated than the main dwelling.

It is a flexible space that can accommodate communal family activities. By simplyfing the design of the new building, only 40 percent of the plot's total area is occupied.

Due to a minimal built-up area, the desire for open green space can be fulfilled at an optimum level.

Left: A semi-outdoor corridor connects the two main masses on the ground floor.

Pavilion 26 houses two main rooms on the ground floor, a dining room and a pantry inside the dining room. These rooms have been designed without borders so they can easily adapt to the family's needs. The ground floor has access to the green open space outside, both visually and physically, through glass pivoting doors. The building's transparency and openness is an answer to the owner's need to maintain control of activity within the pavilion. The application of operable wood panels on the home's upper mass gives it an enclosed appearance. This upper level houses a multifunctonal room.

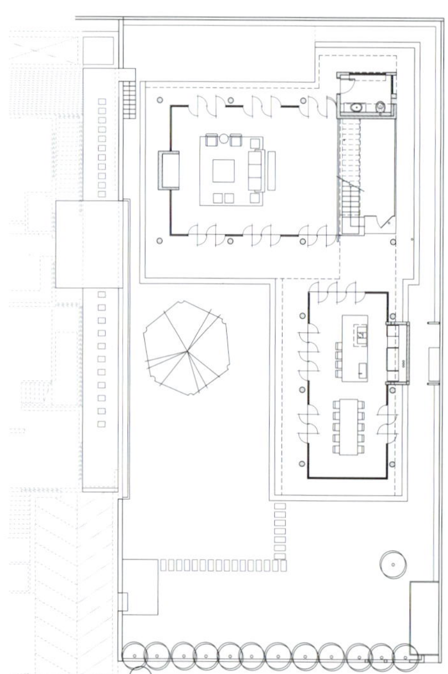

Ground-floor plan

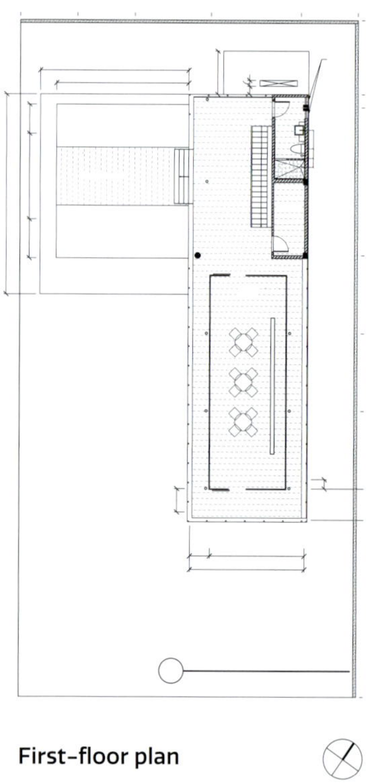

First-floor plan

Top: The building has been set back to provide a green space in the middle of the site. **Opposite top left:** To provide a sense of privacy, the living room is located at the rear of the site. **Opposite top right:** A semi-outdoor corridor connects the two main masses on the ground floor. **Opposite bottom:** Glass walls and pivoting doors reveal the outdoor scenery, allowing occupants to experience the green space from inside the house.

Flexible function as a design concept enables spaces within the home to adapt to the family's various activities. Rooms of the original dwelling, initially intended to accommodate basic communal functions, such as family gatherings and dining, have now adapted to cater for a multitiude of activities, such as aerobics, yoga, business presentations, even retreats and piano recitals. Pavilion 26, initially conceptualized as a supporting building, has now become the hub of family life.

Site Area: 6458 ft^2 (600 m^2) **Floor Area:** 4306 ft^2 (400 m^2) **Photographer:** Sjahrial Iqbal, Mario Wibowo **Design Period:** 2011 **Construction Period:** 2012–2013 **Interior:** Susy Gunawan **Landscape:** Cendrawasih Landscape **Contractor:** ATB Contractor **Structure:** Liman Structure **M&E:** Sitohang Electric **Lighting:** Infinity Lighting

Opposite top: The multifunction room has an open layout, accommodating a variety of activities. **Opposite bottom:** The upper floor is connected to the main house in order to maintain control of the activity happening within the home's pavilion. **Top:** The family can enjoy the night view from the bridge that connects the pavilion and the main house. **Bottom:** The rooftop bridge that connects the upper levels of the house features a walkway decked in wooden materials.

Pramestha Residence

Lembang, West Java
andramatin

Lembang in West Java is well known for its undulating topography and high precipitation. Some areas are precipitous with varying types of soil: from loose, fertile soil to hard, rocky ground. The plot on which the home is located is both precipitous and bounded with a wall of hard, rocky ground, which leans against a hill.

The contoured nature of the plot, with a slope of almost 45 degrees, was a great challenge for the architect. The different land levels were used as a starting point for the home's design and strongly influenced the arrangement of rooms later in the design process. The building's main area has been placed on ground 30 feet (9 meters) above the road in front of it, which gives the home a unique circulation entrance.

To reach the main elevated area, a winding ramp spanning no less than 56 feet (17 meters) on each level was constructed. The ramp was designed as a 5-foot-wide (1.5-meter-wide) corridor and is partly underground and partly aboveground. Even though the circulation to and from the main area ends up taking longer than it would using stairways, the architect opted for the ramp because it considers the elderly, those with disabilities, and baby strollers. Furthermore, a long corridor running in and out of the ground imparts a very impressive spatial experience: oppressive in the beginning but ending in a free and relieving open area.

Left: The house features a jutting mass containing the living spaces, with a roof garden above and lap pool below.

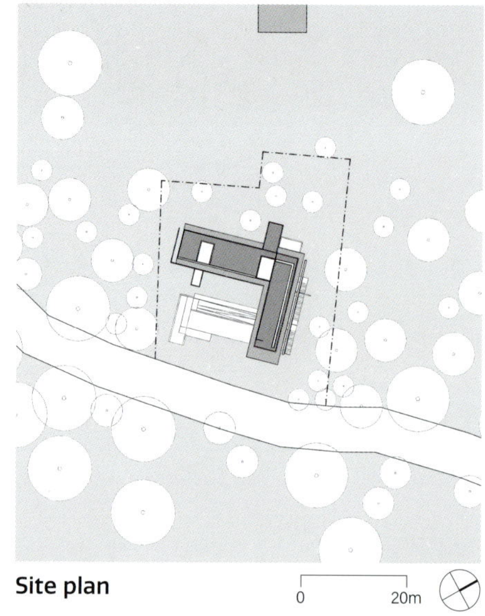

Site plan

This relief from the oppressive feeling imparted by the underground tunnel is enhanced with the surprise of a wide and flat area of grassy lawn, a long swimming pool, and a large box-shaped building covered in filigree. This pleasant surprise is further enhanced with an enchanting view of the valley, which can be enjoyed from the edge of the pool. The altitude of the area gives the edges of this wide flat area a unique atmosphere.

The spatial program of the main, two-story building consists of bedrooms and a living room, which the architect dubbed as a 'wiggle room' for occupants after a long trek along the ramp. The first floor holds the living room on the terrace, the television room, and an open-plan indoor dining room connected to the kitchen. The second floor holds the bedrooms and a study, which have been arranged in an L-shape.

Top left: Concrete is the dominant material used on the main-building mass. Parts of it are covered in roster bricks for shade as well as ventilation. **Bottom right:** Rosters are an ornamental element in this house, set to contrast against the predominantly white interiors. **Opposite top:** The rooms inside the house open up to a striking view of the green hills in Bandung. **Opposite bottom:** The view toward the hill, seen from the house's 'wiggle room'. This area provides relief after traversing the long ramp.

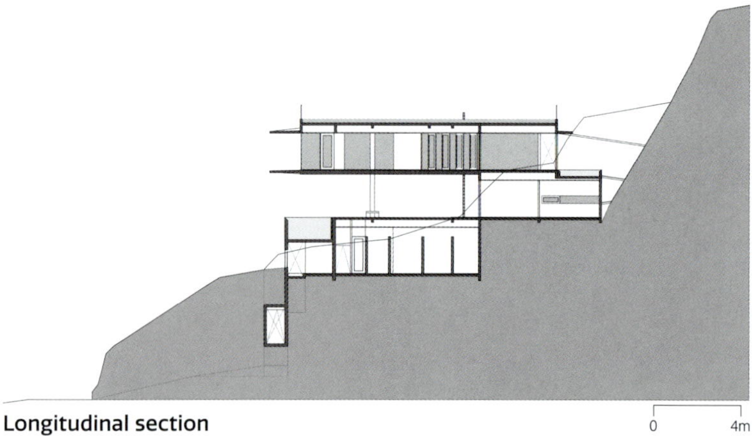

Longitudinal section

A bordering rear wall with wire mesh was designed so that the house could lean against the hill of the site. The surface of this rocky hill has been transformed into an attraction, which can be enjoyed from the interior through sliding-glass doors and large windows. Preserving the unique nature of the plot and constructing the long ramp resulted in an unavoidable increase in construction costs. However, the beautiful scenery and impressively achieved spatial sensations of the Pramestha Residence were well worth it.

Site Area: 13,692 ft^2 (1272 m^2) **Floor Area:** 5802 ft^2 (539 m^2) **Photographer:** Sonny Sandjaya, Sjahrial Iqbal, Mario Wibowo **Design Period:** 2006 **Construction Period:** 2007 **Design Principal:** Andra Matin **Design Team:** Faizal Syamsalam, Irianto B. W., Fandy Gunawan **Landscape:** Karl Princic **Contractor:** Rekamitra, in-house **Structure:** Dani, Hermanto **Lighting:** andramatin

Opposite bottom: The bedroom was designed in close proximity to the natural cliff wall. **Left:** The dramatic experience of living beside a hill is strongly expressed in this house, with a building that 'steps back' and highlights its surrounding steep contours. **Above:** The long ramp functions as the main circulation leading to the main building. The lack of natural lighting is offset with muted lights on the ceiling and the floor of the ramp.

Prashanti Villa

Gianyar, Bali

Arte Architects & Associates

The exotic beaches and unique traditional culture Bali is known for has been encapsulated in Prashanti Villa. Due to the site's beach location. The architect wanted to optimize views of the sea while taking into consideration the extreme weather associated with the region. With a temperature that reaches over 80°F (27°C), smooth air circulation was a priority in the home's design. Thankfully, the client requested a traditional home, designed in accordance with tropical climates. The resulting building blends in with nature and incorporates the peaceful, spiritual characteristics of Bali into its spatial experience.

In order to adapt to parts of the Balinese culture, the *angkul-angkul* (traditional entrance gate) has been set alongside the carport. This wooden gate has been engraved with traditional Balinese patterns. It does not offer an immediate entrance to the home; instead, a privacy wall—*aling-aling in* Balinese—is located just beyond the gate and camouflages activity within the compound. From the *aling-aling*, a footpath running alongside the house enters into a *natar* (courtyard).

Left: The thatched *limasan* (the pyramidal-shaped roof) reflects a traditional Balinese sense of ambience. The trees that grow around the pool emphasize the home's tropical atmosphere.

The house itself consists of three masses, which sit separately on the ground, allowing a pond to flow through the spaces in-between. The main mass, according to Balinese tradition, is the *umah meten*, the sleeping pavilion for the head of the family. The second mass has been designed to house the living room, dining room, and three other bedrooms. These two masses are located perpendicular to one another, leaving a space in the corner for a small family temple made completely of stones. Moreover, a pond connects these three masses. Stepping-stones and a terrace have been incorporated into the pond, allowing occupants to wander to and from each mass. Finally, the whole compound is positioned to face the center of the courtyard, where there is a swimming pool and a floating gazebo.

Opposite top left: A traditional Balinese gate marks the entrance. **Opposite top right:** Landscape design is an important feature of the home. A pond leads to the family temple, which has been placed in higher level to honor the sacredness of the space. **Opposite bottom:** The swimming pool was designed so that occupants can fully enjoy the outdoors. The space includes daybeds and *bale kambang*, a small pavilion for communal activities. **Top:** The semi-public area does not have a defining wall. This allows fluidity with other rooms and the surrounding landscape. **Bottom left & bottom right:** The master bedroom pavilion consists of three separate spaces: the living area, bedroom, and bathroom. The bedroom enjoys an extensive view of the whole compound.

Each pavilion was designed to sit higher than the courtyard, granting occupants a view of the sea beyond the perimeter wall. The architect left the living room pavilion open with no walls, with the different level acting as its only border. In addition to an enhanced visual experience, this openness helps to unify the built space with nature. It consists only of wood columns that support a roof made of *alang-alang*, a material used to build traditional houses. Enclosed behind the living room, a bathroom topped with a glass-roof skylight merges with a small courtyard, creating a natural ambience.

The main sleeping pavilion is made up of bamboo walls, which enhance a sense of privacy. In contrast, large openings at the front sides of the mass allow plenty of sunshine to enter and provide occupants with a view of the whole courtyard. A mediation room and spacious bathroom flank the bed. From the mediation space, occupants have a view of the family temple, which enhances serenity and ambience during meditation. Similar to the bathrooms in the living room pavilion, the main bathroom is enclosed with stonewalls. A gap between the roof and walls make the space feel like a small courtyard closely linked to nature.

Varying materials have been used to enhance the home's natural nuances. The wooden floors and stonewalls; to the engraved decorative elements demonstrate the architect's consistency in maintaining the traditional. Beautifully combined with other materials such as the marble floorings and glass openings, the architect has succeeded in delivering a harmonic dialogue between the modern and traditional.

Top: The living area is located in the middle of the site, providing views of both the swimming pool and the sea. **Middle & bottom:** Each bathroom in the house has been individually designed and each retains the principle of bathing in open air. **Opposite bottom:** The house uses predominantly natural materials, such as wood and stone.

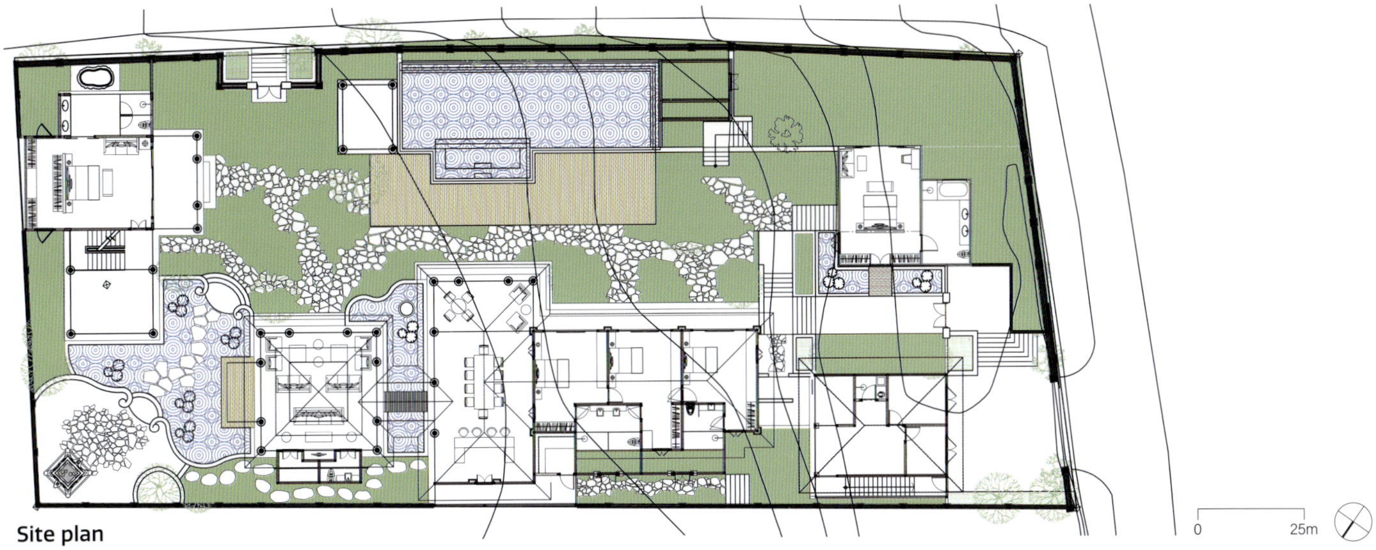

Site plan

Site Area: 18,266 ft² (1697 m²) **Floor Area:** 4252 ft² (395 m²) **Photographer:** Sonny Sandjaya **Design Period:** 2011 **Construction Period:** 2013
Design Principal: Ketut Arthana **Design Team:** Wayan Lanstiaga Satwika, Giuseppe Tatriele, Lahra Tatriele **Contractor:** Ketut Aryadnyana
Structure: Ketut Aryadnyana **M&E:** Ketut Widiantara **Lighting:** Mauro Raffellini Mananara s.r.l.

RD House

Surabaya, East Java
Paulus Setyabudi Architect

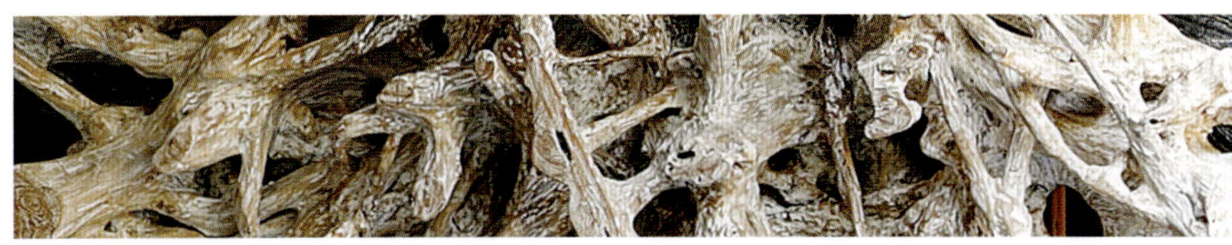

The construction of housing complexes in today's world is inevitable. Typically, housing units only allow interior modification, with few allowing exterior alterations.

Fortunately, some housing complexes do grant the liberty to design a unit in its lot without any restrictions. RD House sits uniquely among other units in a housing complex located in Surabaya.

The unit has been designed in a rotated U-shape mass configuration, creating an inner courtyard and resulting in a slimmer building overall. To accommodate for the owner's bountiful space requirements, the unit has been arranged into a compact three-level home with an elevated entrance, with the ground level functioning as a semi-basement service area. This arrangement generates a living area that is concentrated in the subsequent floors along with an elevated inner courtyard on the second level.

Left: Inner courtyard consisting of a lap pool and small stretch of greenery.

1 Carport
2 Garage
3 Service
4 Entrance
5 Foyer
6 Family room
7 Office
8 Dining room
9 Bedroom
10 Master bathroom
11 Terrace
12 Swimming pool
13 Children's bedroom
14 Sitting room
15 Guest bedroom
16 Playing room
17 Balcony

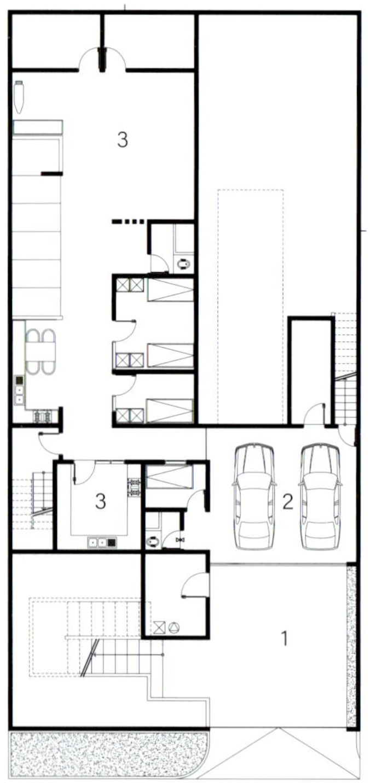

Ground-floor plan

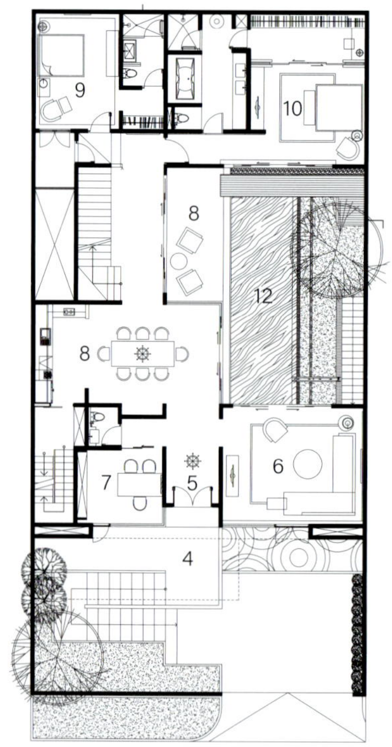

First-floor plan

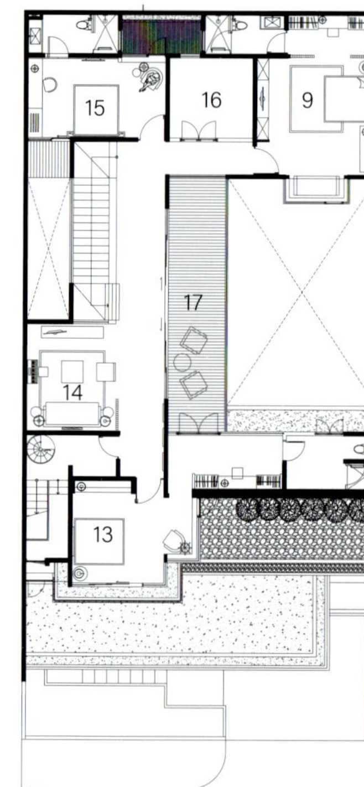

Second-floor plan

RD House

Despite the common association of compact design with cramped space, the architect was able to convey spaciousness through floor-to-ceiling openings in multiple sides of the home. It is thanks to the U-shape configuration that these openings are possible. The U-shape produces more superficies than a conventional rectangular form. These openings—bounded by glass partitions—blur the spatial confines that mainly contribute to the spaciousness. Additionally, the use of light-colored material in the interior elevates the extensive impression of the compact setting, while the natural stone texture of the same material serves as a subtle transition from the interior space to the enclosed private garden.

Consisting of a lap pool and a small stretch of tropical greenery, this man-made sanctuary is the main reason for the aforementioned mass configuration. Essential to contributing an ample amount of natural light into the house, the inner courtyard also provides a beautiful vista for the dining area, living room, and master bedroom on the related floor, as well as the children's bedrooms and balcony on the floor above. Due to the home's northwest and southeast orientation, the high temperature following the imminent direct sunlight is moderated by the presence of the garden, which also casts unique shadows on the terrace by the pool. The open space further triggers air movement, reducing the need for air conditioning inside the house.

Opposite: The master bedroom faces the inner courtyard. **Left:** The mass configuration enables the house to have many openings, especially oriented toward the inner court.

The incorporation of natural elements into the residence doesn't apply to the courtyard alone. In addition to the staircase that connects the main and upper level, a void topped with a skylight penetrates directly through the ground level, illuminating the area that has the least natural light exposure. Additional greenery and water elements embellish the home's front façade. Enveloped within natural materials such as varying stone finishes and wooden partitions, the façade's modern appearance emphasizes the home's affinity with nature.

Not only has the architect managed to integrate natural elements within a very limited land surface, he has also successfully translated the client's requirements and produced a superiorly designed home within the monotonous atmosphere of a housing complex.

Bottom: Full-length openings allow natural ventilation into the spaces, as well as vegetation elements such as the tall grass. **Opposite:** Natural elemenets, such as greenery, wood, and stone materials have been used on the front façade.

Site Area: 4844 ft² (450 m²) **Floor Area:** 8073 ft² (750 m²) **Photographer:** Sonny Sandjaya **Design Period:** 2011–2012 **Construction Period:** 2012–2015 **Design Principal:** Paulus Setyabudi **Design Team:** Yohannes, Elok **Interior:** Valdy Wijaya **Landscape:** Diah Komang **Contractor:** Bambang Handoko **Structure:** Bambang Handoko **M&E:** Bambang Handoko, Dicky Harijanto **Lighting:** Christian Lighting

O.282

Sommerset House

Surabaya, East Java
Das Quadrat

Located on 15,069 square feet (1400 square meters) of land, this generously sized site meant that the clients' spatial needs could be easily fulfilled. The home comprises one main bedroom, a guestroom, and supplementary rooms, such as a yoga studio, hobby room, and a home theatre. Aside from the spatial requirements, the clients also requested that feng shui be incorporated into the home's design. Feng shui involves certain rules and configurations relating to natural elements, and in the case of Sommerset House, the design focused closely on the surrounding nature.

One of the most noticeable natural elements is the 5059-square-foot (470-square-meter) open-garden area surrounding the mass. The garden creates distance between the house and the public road for privacy. Large trees and bushes have been placed in accordance with feng shui. They also block views of passers-by into the house. A distinct use of wood on the home's exterior design complements the greenery.

Composed alongside the predominantly curvilinear white motif is a wooden upper mass, formed by dark-colored wooden panels. The same wooden panels have also been used as flooring for the home's front porch. In addition, a small waterway makes its way along the front porch, framing the porch, before it disappears from sight toward a pond at the back of the house.

Left: The entranceway has been designed as a wooden-floored terrace, framed with a waterway, which showcases a combination of natural materials.

Sommerset House

The concept of unifying the indoor space with the exterior is demonstrated throughout the home's design. Continuing from the outside porch, similar wood-planked flooring maps the interior's main circulation. Spanning from south to north, this circulation becomes the home's backbone. A dry garden on the east side of the house emphasizes this unifying concept. The dry garden is made visible from the inside space through a span of glass walls. A line of white pebbles borders the dry garden's grassy ground. Even inside the house, the same white pebbles have been used as a floor covering in the middle area of the house. A wooden staircase and stonewalled elevator, which lead to the void of the floor above, are situated upon the pebbled flooring. A skylight placed directly above this void allows abundant sunlight to shower inside, further emphasizing a feeling of being outside while inside.

Left: The first zone of the house consists of a living room. A glass door delineates the area from more private areas. **Above:** Stairs and an elevator become the house's vertical circulation. The use of natural materials invites nature inside the house.

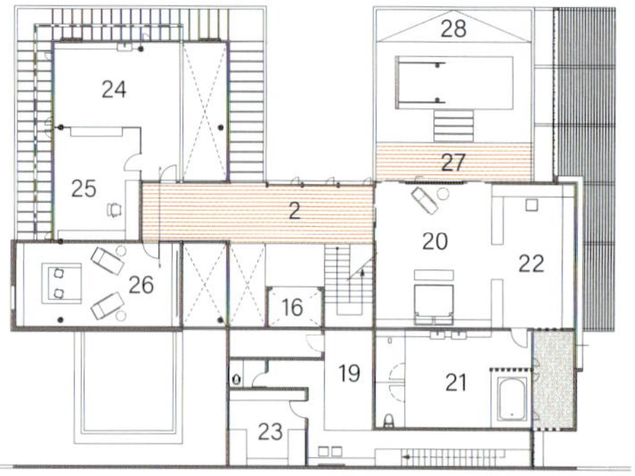

First-floor plan

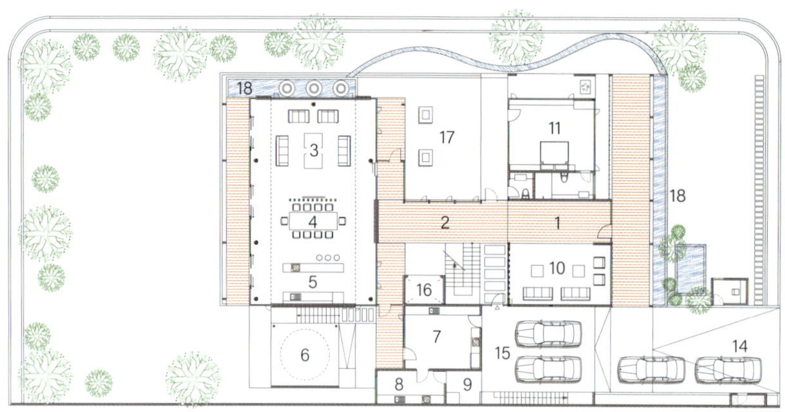

Ground-floor plan

1 Foyer
2 Corridor
3 Living
4 Dining
5 Pantry
6 Yoga
7 Kitchen
8 Wet area
9 Washing area
10 Guest lounge
11 Guest bedroom
12 Powder room
13 Guest bathroom
14 Carport
15 Inner carport
16 Lift
17 Dry garden
18 Pond
19 Washing/drying
20 Master bedroom
21 Master bathroom
22 Walk-in closet
23 Office
24 Hobby area
26 Home theatre
27 Terrace
28 Roof garden

Situated at the far end of the house is the biggest room, which comprises a kitchen/dining room on the west and a living room on the east. Antithetical to the home's front façade, which only shows small openings, the backside of the house boldly opens itself out to an extensive garden. Wide glass openings blur the boundary between the inside space and the garden—another implementation of an intimate relation to the outside environment. Similar to the front façade, a wooden porch running along the back of the house acts as a transitional space between inside and outside.

The intimate relations created with the natural environment have also been applied to the upper floor. Designated as the clients' private space, the master bedroom has exclusive access to a rooftop garden. A lounging area within this space directs views toward lush greenery. Wood-plank flooring has been used for the lounging area and is surrounded by white pebbles. The same curvilinear patterns used on the home's ground exterior have been used as the lounging area's partition, further marking the relation between this secluded area and other spaces of the house.

Opposite bottom: The dry rooftop garden is equipped with a canopy for the occupants' comfort while they enjoy the private scenery. **Top left & bottom:** The family room, dining room, and pantry enjoy views toward the greenery outside. **Top right:** White pebbles and marble have been used in the bathroom, once again bringing natural elements into the interior.

Site Area: 15,069 ft^2 (1400 m^2) **Floor Area:** 10,010 ft^2 (930 m^2) **Photographer:** Sonny Sandjaya **Design Period:** 2012 **Construction Period:** 2013–2015 **Design Principal:** Aditya Tan, Enoch Muljono **Design Team:** Ardhian Ardhi, Arif Amreta **Interior:** Cahya Hening MP, Andi Rian Abdhikara **Landscape:** Rosario Garden Surabaya **Contractor:** AHAY General Contractor Surabaya **Structure:** AHAY General Contractor Surabaya, Casa Interni **M&E:** Jaya Mulya Lighting (Wibisono Surabaya) **Lighting:** Das Quadrat

Songket House

Padang, West Sumatra
Imelda Akmal

Merantau, which means migrating for a new life away from home, is a tradition of the Minangkabau people in West Sumatra. Every holiday season they visit their extended family's traditional home, called a *rumah gadang*, to reunite with their family. While the tradition of reuiniting with family is still present in modern-day culture, returning to the traditional home is not as prevalent. This is the case with the owner of Songket House who, after migrating from Minangkabau to Jakarta, wanted a home to gather with his extended family in Padang city during the holidays.

Padang is located on the south coast of the West Sumatra province. There is no particular dwelling typology rooted in the province's capital except for an adaptation of the horn-like curved roof—typically found on *rumah gadang*—in modern buildings and buildings with classic European style. This condition prompted the architect to respond through a 'silent', contemporary design, which would boast firm and clean geometric lines to grab people's attention. A design with basic shape composition is unfamiliar to most Padang people, including the owner's wife who expressed her initial resistance toward the idea.

Left: The *pucuk rebung* motif of West Sumatra's *songket* woven cloth has been applied as the motif of the entry foyer's surface.

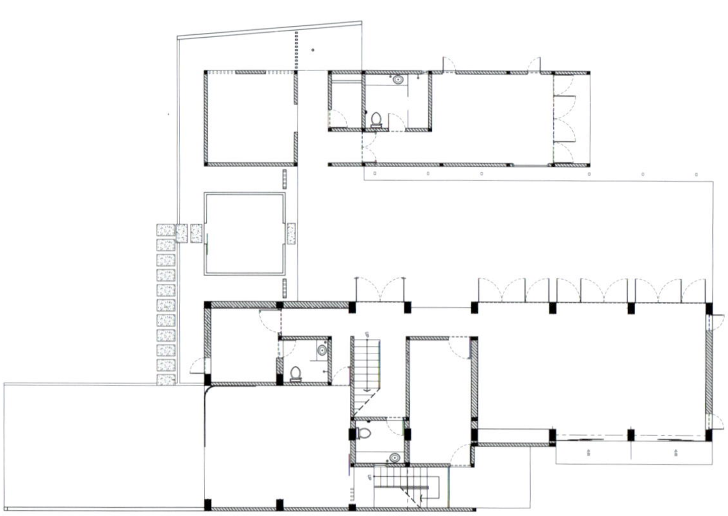

Ground-floor plan

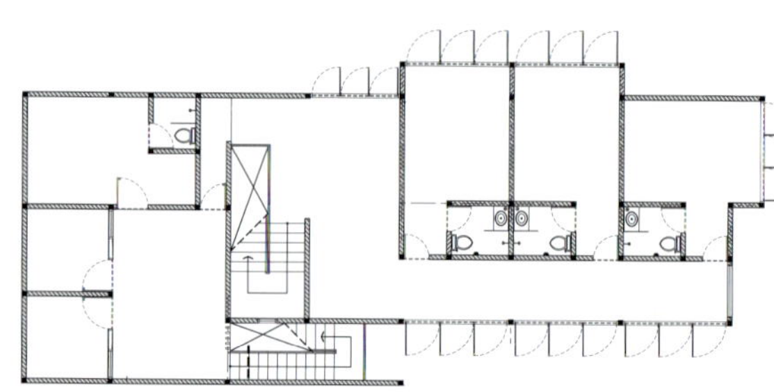

First-floor plan

Songket House

Opposite top: The façade has a silent design, with minimum openings and ornaments. **Bottom:** The semi-outdoor terrace provides an additional space to accommodate the reception of a large number of guests.

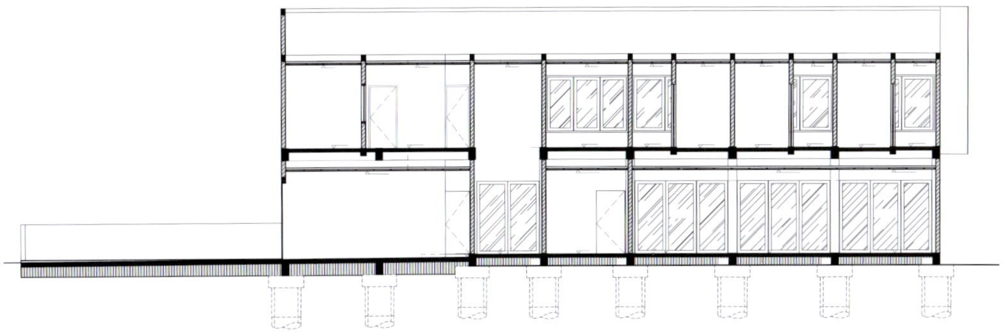

Longitudinal section

Despite this resistance, the contemporary shape and spatial programming of the house went ahead. The owner desired a huge house in which he could host a large number of guests. The architect responded to this request by separating the private area and public area on the ground floor into two main buildings. The building on the left is intended for tranquil activites and comprises the main bedroom and praying room. Meanwhile, the inertactive area, comprising the living room and dining room, is located within the larger building mass on the right and boasts an open-plan design.

A semi-outdoor terrace becomes the intermediary space between the two main buildings. Folding glass doors directly connect the terrace with the living room and the dining room. The terrace also serves as an extended space for the inside rooms. This provided a solution to the homeowner's need for an expansive area in which to welcome a large number of guests. The terrace is a statement of the architect, who believes that people who live in tropical climates should interact with outdoor spaces. However, it was not an easy task convincing the owner to apply this outdoor interaction. The owner had spent years living in an air-conditioned house, and the outdoor interaction concept was unfamiliar. As a result, this semi-outdoor terrace became the biggest compromise reached between the owner and architect.

Another factor that affected the form and layout of the building's masses was the owner's desire for no fence. This prompted the architect to find a solution for overcoming potential security issues. This came in the form of a massive façade.

The architect also designed an entry foyer between the two main buildings, which functions as a shield to conceal the semi-outdoor terrace from outsider eyes. The entry foyer is surrounded by a pond. The water element has aesthetic value but also acts as a security measure, preventing strangers from trespassing through the gap between the masses.

The shape of entry foyer exhibits a box-like form, similar to that of the main masses but with a metal material. In line with its function to welcome guests, the foyer appears to be more open through perforated openings. The architect selected *pucuk rebung*, a motif typically found on *songket* woven cloth of West Sumatra, to be adapted onto the entry foyer's façade. The choice was made by the architect in an effort to provide a sense of belonging to the owners. The *songket* woven cloth pattern has also been applied to ornaments in the home's interior.

The architect's endeavor to create occupant interaction with outdoor spaces was materialized. The terrace maintains a comfortable temperature due to the occasional blowing wind and most of the owners activities are conducted within this space. The design of Songket House is unlike anything the residents of Padang have seen before. It introduces a completely new typology of dwelling to the area.

Top: The details of the entry foyer and the pond, which both serve as security measures. **Bottom:** The living room directly connects to the outdoor space through massive glass doors. **Opposite:** Wooden panels become the pergola's secondary roof and provide shade for the semi-outdoor terrace.

Site Area: 9688 ft² (900 m²) **Floor Area:** 4004 ft² (372 m²) **Photographer:** Sonny Sandjaya **Design Period:** 2012–2013 **Construction Period:** 2013–2014 **Landscape:** Imelda Akmal **Structure:** Edinoy Sahdie **M&E:** Edinoy Sahdie

Spiral House

Surabaya, East Java
Ivan Priatman Architecture

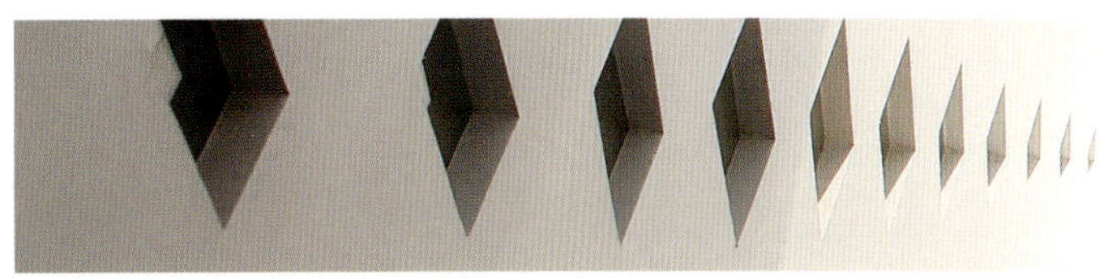

This house is located in a housing complex on the western fringe of Surabaya. The city of Surabaya is located on the north-eastern side of Java Island, approximately 475 miles (765 kilometers) from the capital city of Jakarta. Surabaya is situated near one of Indonesia's largest harbors. The city possesses the special characteristics of a tropical seaside city—windy with intense sunlight during the day.

These climatic conditions prompted the owner to request that the architect incorporate a courtyard into the design of the house. In addition to providing a sheltered outdoor area, the courtyard ensures privacy while allowing occupants to indulge in open-air activities. It also creates a permeable relationship between exterior and interior spaces. Most importantly, the courtyard creates its own cooling microclimate due to open space beneath the shadow of the building.

The architect wanted to incorporate the concept of spatial continuity into the home's design. This continuity is translated through a combination of linear spatial organisations coupled with a hierarchical arrangement from the most public service areas and the foyer, to the most private areas, such as the master bedroom. This spatial organisation and massing resulted in the house becoming elongated and narrow. Incidentally, the architect had to adapt this design to a wide square-shaped site, measuring a total of 4994 square feet (464 square meters).

Left: The house is located on a corner site, which made protection from the weather and privacy more difficult.

In order to resolve the aforementioned design issues, the architect decided to bend the elongated and narrow mass of the building. At the ground floor, the mass bends to follow the shape of the site, while on the first floor the bending takes the twisting form of a triangle, which allows a courtyard to take shape in the middle of the house. These two types of bending and twisting create a helical circulation twice around the site. This forms a unique spiralled space, thus informing the name of the house.

Apart from the courtyard and the continuity spatial programme, the architect responded to design requirements through careful consideration of the wind direction and sun angle. This consideration was particularly important as hot and humid tropical weather results in intense sunshine throughout the year. The home's design avoids the direct morning and evening sun but welcomes the prevailing wind flow.

The architect designed a block mass wall on the western elevation and generous openings on the eastern elevation, which allow morning sunlight into the house. Large plants placed outside of this façade filter and calm the intensity and heat of the sunlight. The plants provide shadows and a cooling effect while acting as a curtain to prevent direct views from the outside of the house. A reflecting pool located on the eastern façade helps to reduce heat intensity and gives the home a soothing temperature, especially on the east façade.

Opposite: The pond and plants on the east façade create a cooling microclimate for the house.
Bottom left & right: Light slats on the staircase connect the spiral rooms with the massive blank thermal wall.

Above: Wooden parquet strips create a homely feel. **Opposite bottom left:** The east façade has large openings to allow for morning light. The pool and vegetation help reduce heat and glare. **Opposite bottom right:** The bedrooms are furnished with full-length windows that overlook greenery.

The architect chose to design the form of the house with strong and modern geometries. The plastered, white painted walls emphasize the feeling of modern minimalism. This is in stark contrast to the approach of a conventional tropical building, which would normally possess a sloping roof with large overhangs to protect the walls and openings from harsh sunlight and rain. This unique approach could be successfully executed due to modern building technologies, such as a high performance painting system, which better protects the walls from arduous sunlight and rain for a longer period of time. Door and window openings include waterproofed, self-draining seals. The geometric shape possesses strong, clean, and sleek lines, which emphasize the unique identity of the house.

Clean and sleek geometry has also been applied to the home's interior design and furniture. White painted, plastered walls feature throughout, with complementary color combinations for the furniture and kitchen. The interior floors are made of wooden parquet strips, which give a sense of warmth of the house.

Spiral House has been designed with careful consideration for the tropical climate, proving that 'tropical' is not only a style but also a design solution. Style, in the opinion of the architect, should only be applied once all climatic elements have been adequately considered and designed.

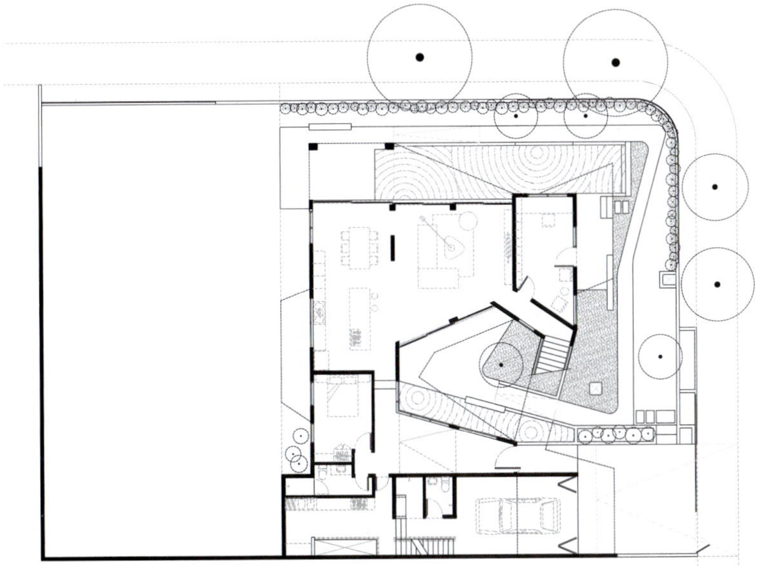

Ground-floor plan

First-floor plan

Site Area: 4994 ft² (464 m²) **Floor Area:** 4413 ft² (410 m²) **Photographer:** Ivan Priatman **Design Period:** 2010–2011 **Construction Period:** 2011–2013
Design Principal: Ivan Priatman **Design Team:** Iwan Andijanto **Interior:** Ivan Priatman Architecture
Contractor: Tycon **Structure:** Ratno **M&E:** Ivan Priatman Architecture

Stilt House at Pramestha

Lembang, West Java, Indonesia
Tan Tik Lam Architects

The highest point of the site is level with the road, with the remaining area descending into a steep slope. This slope leans down toward a valley, which makes it invisible from the road. The architect decided to utilize the nature of the site by creating a building mass that aligns with the land's typography, leaning vertically downward. This approach results in the home appearing as a single-story building. Its four additional levels below are not apparent from the road.

The architect wanted to avoid the use of a large massing on the land. As a result, two separate masses have been constructed on the 30,139-square-foot (2800-square-meter) site, with primary and service functions divided into each. By utilizing this method, the respective building mass becomes smaller and lighter. This reduces ground loads and addresses the risks associated with sloping, unstable land. By minimizing the contiguity between the building and ground, the architect was able to preserve the sloping nature of the land. This was achieved by raising the home upon board piles. These bear the weight of the piles, blocks, and the building's floor. The pile structure and small building mass reduce the risk of the building shifting with soil movements if a landslide were to occur.

Left: The house occupies a steep hillside, resulting in a mass with truncated levels.

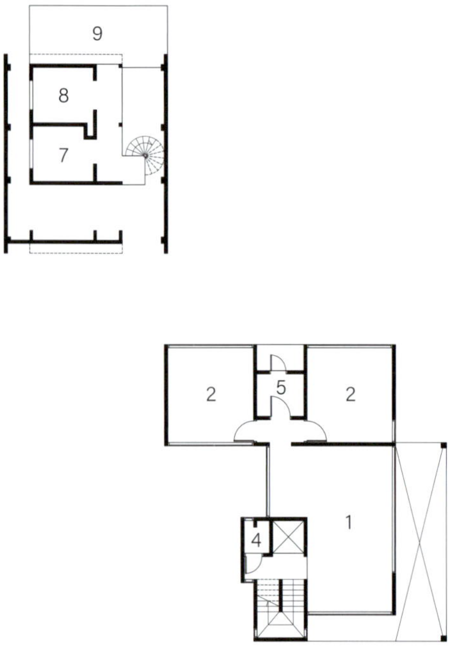

Basement floor plan

Ground-floor plan

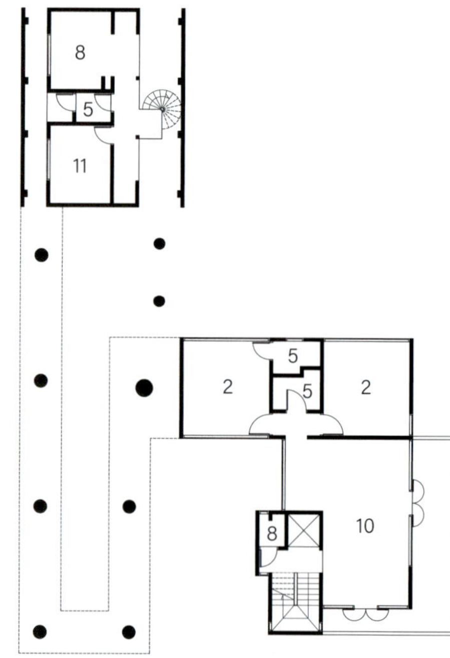

First-floor plan

Stilt House at Pramestha

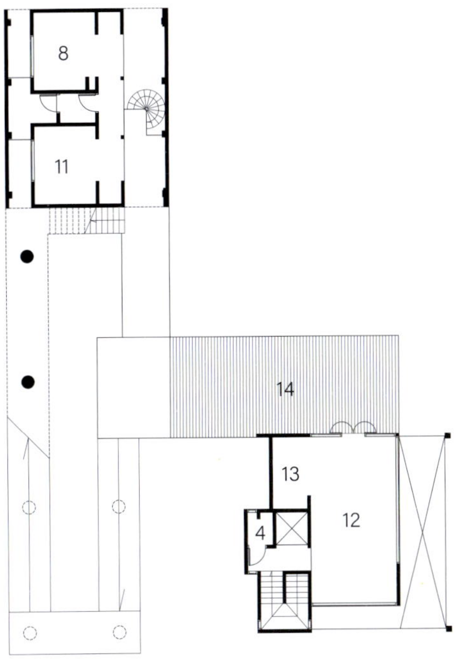

Second-floor plan

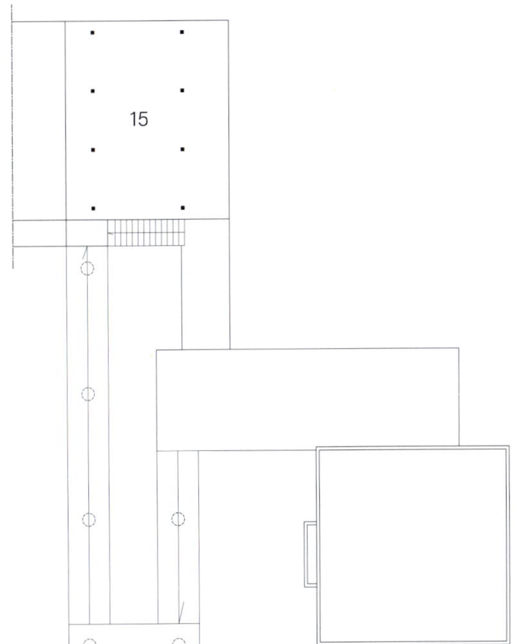

Third-floor plan

1 Study
2 Bedroom
3 Wardrobe
4 WC
5 Bathroom
6 Pool
7 Laundry
8 Storage
9 Drying area
10 Living room
11 Maid's room
12 Dining room
13 Pantry
14 Wood deck
15 Carport

0 4m

The effort to minimize the contiguity with the ground has also been applied to the home's circulation paths, particularly between the front road and main building. The architect designed a roofless, outdoor ramp, which is supported by the thinnest possible steel stilts. Steel was chosen in order for the stilts to make the lightest possible contact with the ground. This circulation route takes the form of a ramp and therefore required a longer pathway. It creates a splendid experience for occupants, allowing them to breath in the clean, fresh mountainous air and be at one with the surrounding nature. The end of the path meets a wall-less, wooden-floored reception balcony, which boasts a magnificent view of the surrounding hills and valley. The transition from the circulation path to the balcony provides occupants with a well-rounded and memorable spatial experience.

Opposite: A scenic view of the surrounding nature gives the reception balcony a refreshing visual experience.
Left: The bored-pile foundation supporting the ramp reveals the empty space below the building—a result of the stilt house structure.

Along with a reception balcony, each floor of the home enjoys scenic views from balconies and through retractable windows. The broad dimensions and lined-up placement of the windows promote clean air circulation throughout the home.

The commitment of architect to minimize obstruction to the existing terrain allows Stilt House to exist in harmony with the natural surrounds.

Top left: Wide openings in most of the home's spaces allow for optimum light and the circulation of fresh air. **Top right:** The double-height ceiling of the balcony creates a wide 'frame' for the scenery of the surroundings. **Bottom:** A pool on the ground floor adjoins the steeply sloping land. **Opposite:** A view of the building from the opposite hill. The pale expression of the building creates a contrast with the green surroundings.

Site Area: 30,139 ft² (2800 m²) **Floor Area:** 7104 ft² (660 m²) **Photographer:** Sonny Sandjaya, Sjahrial Iqbal, Mario Wibowo **Design Period:** 2007
Construction Period: 2008–2010 **Design Principal:** Tan Tik Lam **Design Team:** Priesto Naray, Immanuel Candra **Interior:** Era Said
Landscape: Intaran Design **Structure:** SRS 51 **Lighting:** Lighting Design System

Tamarind House

Lebak Bulus, South Jakarta
d-associates architect

Tamarind House is a private residence situated on a 24,757 square feet (2300 square meters) of land, in a gated residential development area in South Jakarta, Indonesia. The spacious compound itself occupies the west end of the land, which is surrounded by the Pesanggrahan River and tamarind trees. Given the site's characteristics, the Jakarta-based architecture studio d-associates delivered a tropical meets modern-style elegance design.

When dealing with a tropical climate people living in the Southeast Asia region unsurprisingly enjoy the merging of indoor and outdoor space because of the emphasis on natural light and ventilation. This is in line with one of the principles of modern architecture, which encourages transparency and openness as a fundamental design feature. Thus, the modern tropical design of Tamarind House enables an optimum relationship with nature, which supports occupant activity through maximum openings. In the case of Tamarind House, the architects translated this approach in the form of expansive floor-to-ceiling windows. The windows double as large pivoted folding doors and can be opened entirely, allowing a generous amount of natural light and air to enter the interior space. Furthermore, they create an unobstructed relationship between indoor and outdoor space.

Left: Each bedroom has a hanging balcony wrapped with a cantilevered wall. Other than protecting the balcony from the rain, it also visually frames the surrounding vista.

Another compelling feature of the house is the series of ramps located on the east side. One ramp wraps entirely around the house and stands out as a strong architectural device. It negotiates intermittent space and creates delightful moments of engagement with the interior as well as the exterior, without compromising the nominal functions of the house. Aside from its function as the only mode of vertical circulation, the ramp layer forms an outer 'skin' for the house, mitigating weather and supporting natural ventilation throughout the building. The ramp provides a continuous sequence from the first floor to the uppermost floor and provides occupants with the opportunity to appreciate nature as they walk through the space. This design feature demonstrates a high degree of spatial and functional innovation through the use of simple architectural elements.

The house consists of two structures: the main house and the service area. The main house is a three-story mass elongated in the north-south axis. This configuration allows the house to obtain a view toward the Pesanggrahan River to the west. The spatial programme of the main house is divided into public and private zones. The first floor—a public zone—hosts three separate areas linked with by a continuous corridor: a living room and a dining room, which extends to a vast terrace and library.

Top: A large sheltering roof, with deep overhangs supported by thin concrete columns, defines the house. **Bottom:** A lengthy ramp leads from level to level and takes up almost a third of the overall building volume. The ramp is exposed to the outdoors but protected by the concrete roof. **Opposite bottom:** Pivoted folding doors blur the boundary between the inside and outside space. This also allows occupants a continuous view of the outdoors.

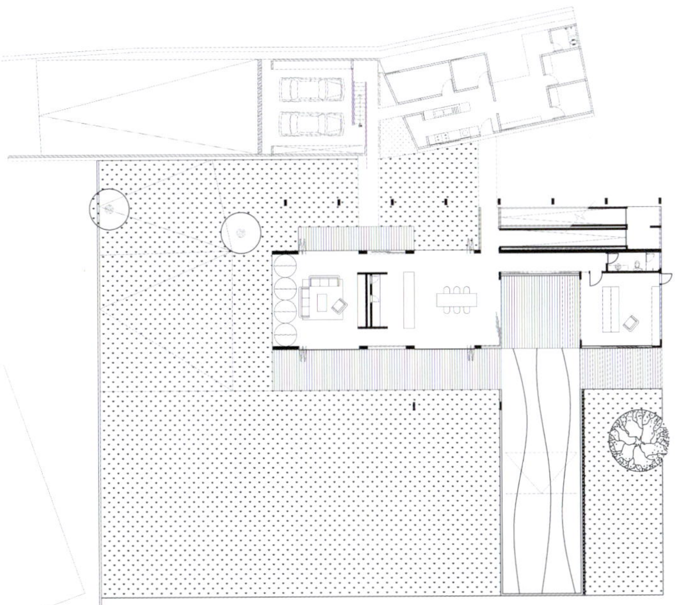

Ground-floor plan

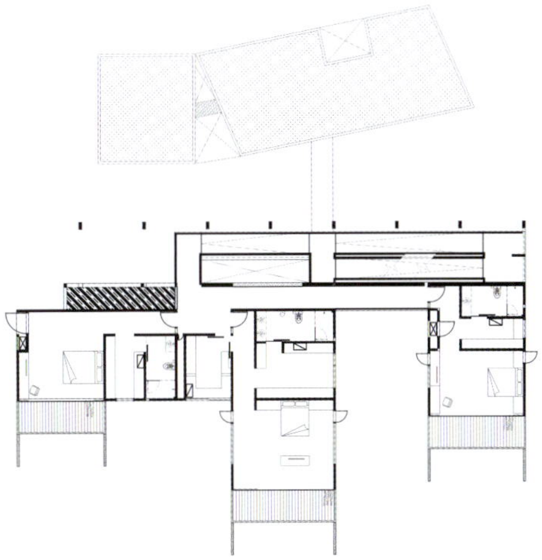

Upper-floor plan

Private areas are located on the upper floor: a private library and work room; the main bedroom, which sits above the dining room; and the children's bedroom, which are located at the far ends above the living room. Each of these rooms has a balcony with an overhang as a shield from rain and direct sunlight.

Similar to the first floor, the rooms on the upper floor are connected by a corridor. Further up, there is a partly shaded roof garden with plenty of vegetation. The roof garden accommodates the family's outdoor activities and allows them to enjoy the surrounding views from a height. In a separate mass, just across the corridor on the first floor, the service area houses the kitchen, maid's bedroom, and a living space.

Despite its monumental appearance, the house adopts a rather neutral color palette coupled with humble materials, which capitalize on mundane architectural details and express its tropical setting. The simple materials help to distinguish different elements of the house. For example, exposed concrete is used for all external walls; concrete rosters are used for the wall of the roof garden; and a timber-slat screen has been used alongside the corridor. This approach to materiality enriches texture and spatial dimensions. Through meticulous design and attention to the client's needs, Tamarind House by d-associates has been beautifully imagined for the family and is a modern delight within the urban tropics.

Opposite top & below: Each bedroom has a hanging balcony wrapped with a cantilevered wall. Other than protecting the balcony from the rain, it also visually frames the surrounding vista. **Opposite middle:** The roof garden is covered in variety of vegetation. White pebbles have been incorporated as a landscape accent, while the wooden deck acts as a subtle spatial demarcation. **Opposite bottom:** A wall of concrete rosters serves as a separator between the ramp and the rooftop area, keeping it hidden from public eyes.

Site Area: 24,757 ft² (2300 m²) **Floor Area:** 14,747 ft² (1370 m²) **Photographer:** Mario Wibowo **Design Period:** 2007–2012 **Construction Period:** 2010–2012 **Design Principal:** Gregorius Supie Yolodi, Maria Rosantina **Design Team:** Sonny Restu Wibowo, Fajar Krisnawan **Landscape:** Nurhafidh D. (Lanskaptika Prima) **Contractor:** Bagos Prihantoro **Structure:** Muchammad Umar **M&E:** Rusman Riadi **Lighting:** Lenny, Lentera Lighting

Three Layers House

Dago Village, Ciburial
Pipih Priyatna Architects

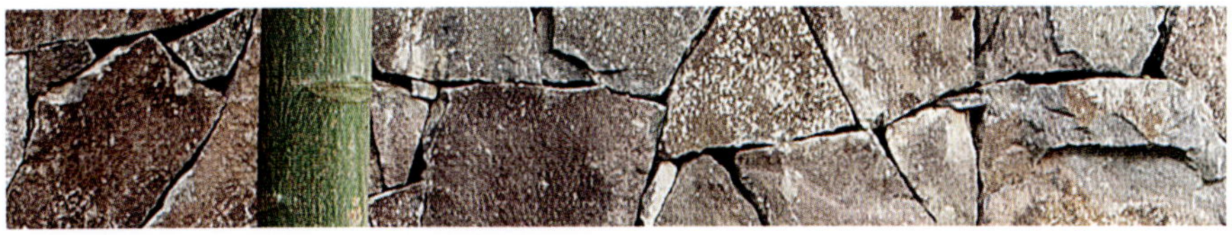

Located just 6 miles (10 kilometers) from Bandung city, Ciburial is a village that still retains a pristine environment. Urban development is yet to peak in the area so it still has ample green space. Within the housing complex in the village, the architect designed a rest house, which sits on a contouring site flanked by two residential roads.

As a rest house, the floorplan of the building is quite simple. It consists of three bedrooms, a guest room, a dining room, and a pantry. The spaces were arranged horizontally by the architect, which formed the building mass into a long, one-story box. At the back of the mass, the architect designed a cantilevered deck, intended as a space to relax and enjoy the view of the vast green hills. The rear of the house is mostly covered with glass walls to ensure that the scenery can be enjoyed from inside the home. The glass walls also give the building a lightweight appearance, which complements the home's simple, clean-white look.

In response to the land's contours, the site is divided into three categories: excavated ground, filled ground, and the ground left hanging on the cliff. This aims to prevent the building mass from concentrating on one point. As a result of land excavation, most of the building sits on even ground. The filled ground has been built into small hills at the northern part of the site.

Left: The house boasts the shape of a simple rectangle with wide openings to attract daylight and natural temperature.

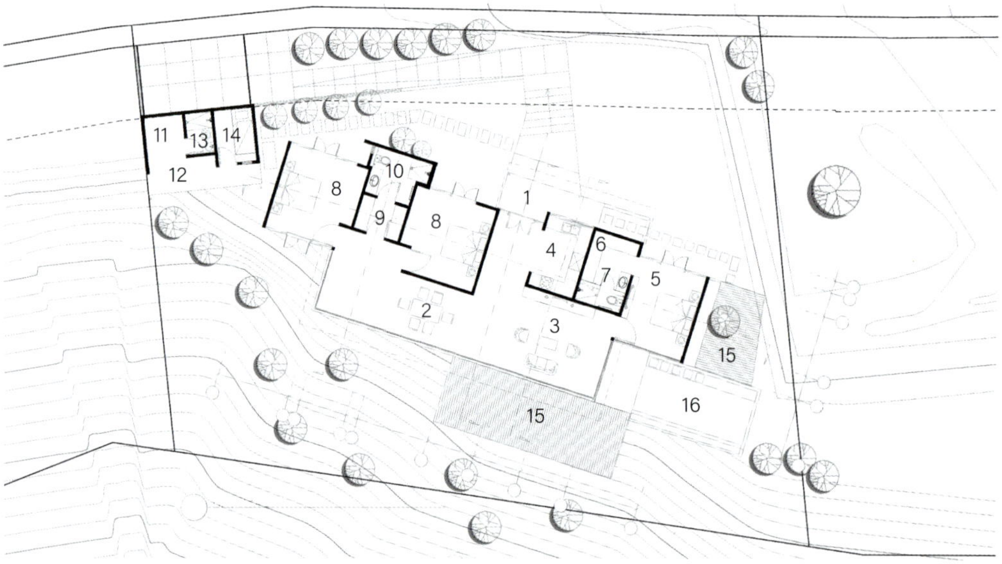

Ground-floor plan

Left: The house overlooks a slope framed by tropical shrubbery beneath. **Right:** The open deck at the back of the house is an additional space equipped with cantilever system hovering over the slope. **Opposite top:** The interior looks out toward its surroundings from a considerable height.

This site distribution eventually determined the type of structure and construction used for each part of the house. A concrete structure has been applied to parts of the flattened ground, while the parts hanging on the hill have been constructed with a stilt system; supported by board piles that are connected to lightweight steel columns.

Aside from the specific structures and construction, careful attention was paid to water absorption on the landscape. According to the architect, the water flow on the contouring site needed to be controlled, with zero run-off and no water flow on the land surface. Rainfall entirely absorbed by the soil also needed to be avoided because excessive water absorption burdens the soil and increases the risk of landslide. Inresponse, the home uses biopore, which expands the space for water absorption on even ground. Instead of applying a system to stem the water flow on the sloping ground, the architect made use of strong-rooted vegetation to reinforce the soil.

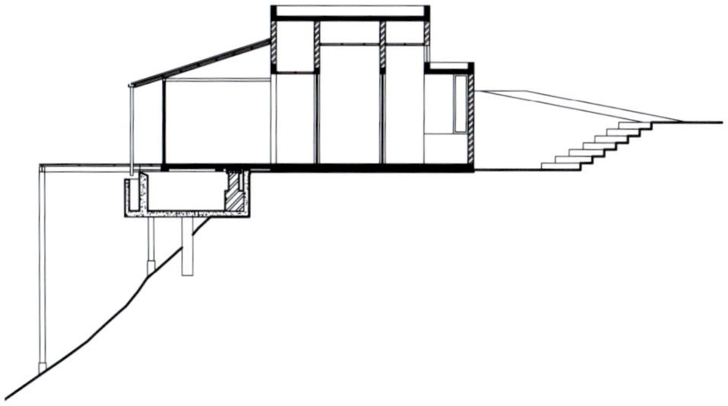

Transverse section

The types of vegetation were chosen carefully. Slow-growing, strong-rooted trees, such as damar trees (native coniferous timber trees), were planted as long-term investments to strengthen the ground structure. In addition, during the early stage of the construction, several fast-growing trees were planted to treat the land and to screen sun heat.

The considerations made by the architect when designing and constructing the house demonstrate that the success of a building on a contouring site can only be achieved when the design maximizes not only scenic beauty but also the longevity of the structure and landscape.

Opposite: The roof garden functions as insulation and an aesthetic element. **Left:** Small valleys in the house's yard are result of soil piled on the excavated part of the site. **Right:** Reinforced soil walls made of river stones have been applied to the main entrance path.

Design Firm: Pipih Priyatna Architects **Location:** Ciburial Village, West Java **Site Area:** 7664 ft² (712 m²) **Floor Area:** 1755 ft² (163 m²) **Photographer:** Sjahrial Iqbal, Mario Wibowo **Design Period:** 2011 **Construction Period:** 2011–2012 **Design Principal:** Pipih Priyatna **Design Team:** Micheline Severina, Desti Ayu **Landscape:** Pipih Priyatna **Contractor:** Pipih Priyatna Contractors **Structure:** Hermanto Subagijo **M&E:** Eddy Prasojo

The Tree House

Denpasar, Bali

Arte Architect & Associates

Balinese architect, Ketut Arthana, always wanted to live in a tree house surrounded by the serenity of nature with his family. A secluded hillside plot in close proximity of a river and natural vegetation was the ideal location. Fortunately, this desired plot existed within the Denpasar area, and despite its urban location, had retained its natural atmosphere.

The architect preserved the pristine condition of the plot as much as possible. Existing tall trees were left to grow naturally. The regulations stipulating the basic building coefficient did not allow the building mass to exceed 30 percent of the total area, and areas 49 feet (15 meters) wide alongside riverbanks were designated as no-build zones. As a result, the architect was left with a significant amount of space that could not be built upon.

Left: In addition to acting as aesthetic and recreational elements, the pool and adjacent water fountains help cool the temperature around the house.

When viewing the home from the road on the west side, the site's topography comes into clear view, with the hillside terracing all the way down to the riverbank on the east side. The architect used these natural terraces as outdoor stairways, connecting the different levels of the site.

In addition to preserving the authenticity of the landscape, the natural terraces have been preserved in order to provide a variation in levels on each floor of the home.[1] The home's reception area is located on the ground floor, which is at the same elevation as the road but level with the branches of surrounding trees. The floors below the ground floor feel more private as they are situated on a cliffside below the surface of the road.

1 Wiryomartono, Bagoes. *The Search for Synergy of Duality: Notes on the Architecture of Ketut Arthana*, 2014.

Top: Ornamental tropical plants have been used as decoration inside and outside of the house. **Bottom:** The slim swimming pool hangs 30 feet (9 meters) aboveground and 69 feet (21 meters) above the river. **Opposite:** Existing vegetation has been left to intervene and grow around the house, creating the desired 'tree-house' appearance.

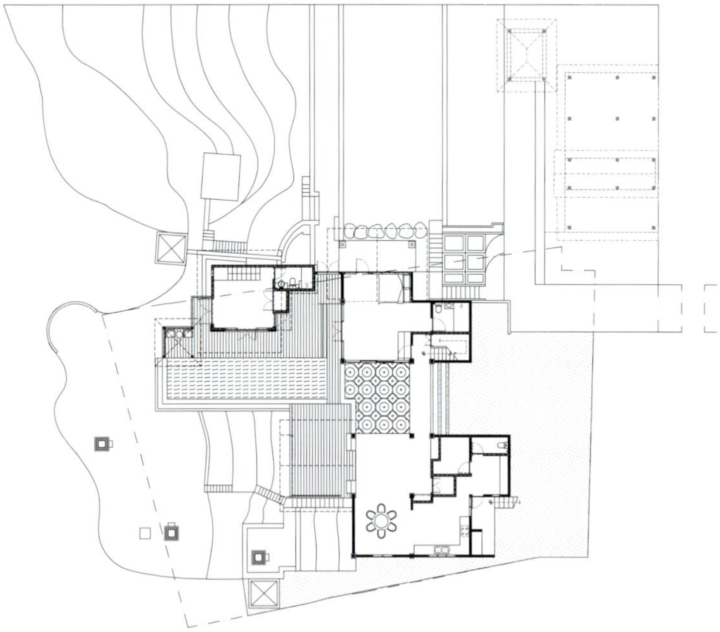

Ground-floor plan

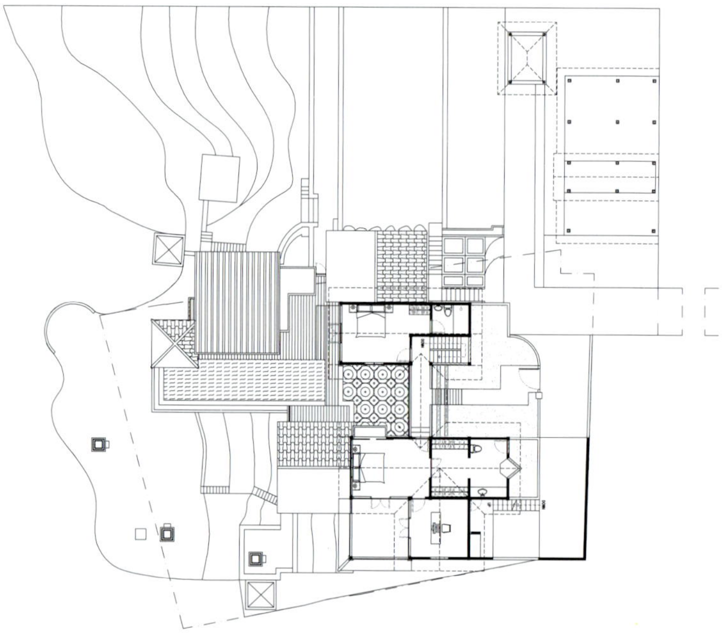

First-floor plan

The Tree House

Upon entering the house, visitors are greeted by a small garden with a path leading to a bridge. This entrance has been deliberately designed to create a feeling of 'entering into nature.' The bridge commands an excellent view of the floors below as well as the forest and river located at the rear of the site.

The home is constructed mostly from worn ironwood taken from old power poles, which has then been connected with Japanese-style joints. This building style, along with the open roof, give the home a sense of simplicity and embody the tree house identity desired by the owner.

The tree house atmosphere is further enhanced by the absence of walls in the living room and on the first floor. From the living room, which is enclosed only by wooden railing, branches of surrounding trees are within arm's reach. Furthermore, some tree branches grow through the roof and wooden deck of the porch, completely immersing the occupants in nature.

Opposite bottom: Natural stone and wooden elements have been used extensively throughout the interior, including the furniture. **Top:** The living room on the ground floor has been designed without walls to enhance the close-to-nature spatial and visual experience. **Bottom:** Emerging from the floorboards, existing trees and vegetation were disturbed as little as possible. The architect incorporated them as part of the house.

Site Area: 13,939 ft² (1295 m²) **Floor Area:** 5097 ft² (473.5 m²) **Photographer:** Sonny Sandjaya **Design Period:** 1991–1992 **Construction Period:** 1992–1993 **Design Principal:** Ketut Arthana **Interior:** Ketut Arthana **Landscape:** Ketut Arthana **Structure:** Arte Architect & Associates **M&E:** Ketut Arthana **Lighting:** Ketut Arthana

Trimmed Reform House

South Tangerang, Banten
SUB

Located within a gated housing complex in South Tangerang, Trimmed Reform House stands on a 2185-square-foot (203-square-meter) corner lot. The compound's eye-catching profile, created by its massive concrete envelope and tapered edges, forms a remarkable ensemble in a suburban context. Budget restrictions and limited area meant the architect had to improvise by using unpretentious materials fused with a modern take on the properties of tropical architecture, in order to create a dramatic design statement.

The restrictive site encouraged the architect to creatively approach the home's spatial arrangement. In response to the site, the least used spatial functions were eliminated, forming a U-shape plan that embraces the inner court. The court serves as a green oasis, pouring daylight into the house. It also offers a pleasant view, reinforces ventinaltion, and reduces thermal heat loads imposed on the home's internal spaces. For the guest bathroom, the architect utilized an empty space tucked away under the stairs. The living room has been designed with an open plan, ensuring fluid circulation and interaction between family and guests. As a multi-functional space, it also has the capacity to act as a communal area during events. A large pivoted glass door allows adequate sunlight and air circulation from the inner court to enter the house. It also blurs the boundary between inside and outside, creating a continuous view from the interior to the exterior.

Left: The interior exudes a comfortable ambience through a combination of different yet cohesive materials in warm tones.

Due to the limited budget, the architect applied several adjustments to design executions and material choice. This included cutting off the height of the initial saddle-roof form to create a continuous flat PVC roof. To address the need for security and privacy, the house was designed with as few openings as possible, essentially turning its back to the street. Consequently, this approach would have resulted in the home appearing as a hefty and enclosed stacked box. With this in mind, the architect designed the western wall as a door that could be fully opened as required, allowing the living room to intersect with the outdoor area, in order for the home to seem more spacious.

When further tackling the home's apperance, the architect implemented a 'tightlacing' concept inspired by the dress reform movement of the Victorian Era, where women used tight bodices to achieve the ideal image of feminine attractiveness. Departing from this idea, the ground floor has been scaled down, making it smaller than the upper floor. This allows the upper-floor plate to function as eaves. Additionally, a few corners of the upper mass were trimmed to demonstrate concept continuity, further emphasizing the building's slim appearance as well as helping it reconcile with the scale and height of its neighbors, while still standing out.

The building's façade gravitates toward a monochromatic color scheme, especially shades of gray and paler tints, alluding to a rough yet modern persona. Predominant splashes of white tones in the living room neutralize the exterior color. Earthy tones from the wooden furnishings, walls, and the floor showcase an elegant simplicity, which radiates a light, airy, and relaxing ambience.

Top: The main entrance has been designed as a gigantic door. When closed, it disguises the wall of the lower mass. **Middle:** The patio in front of the house functions as a social space. **Bottom:** Wide openings toward the inner court allow the house to draw in sufficient natural light and quality ventilation. **Opposite top:** The massive slanted concrete block visually integrates with the surrounding context.

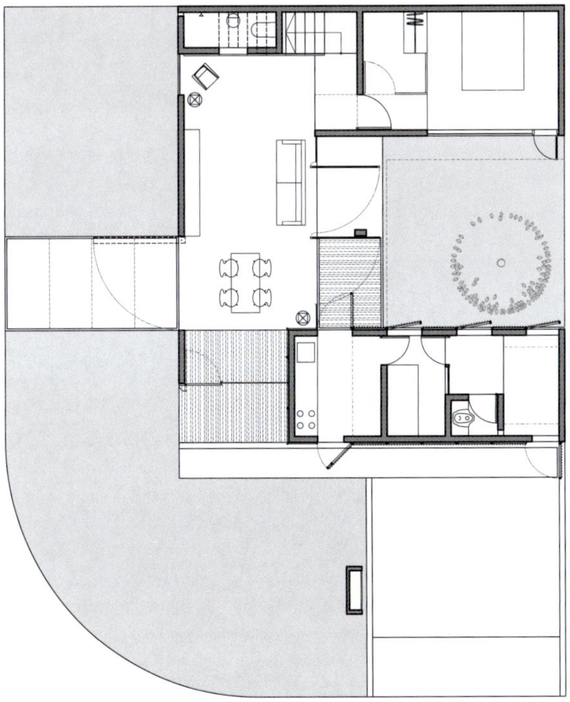

Ground-floor plan

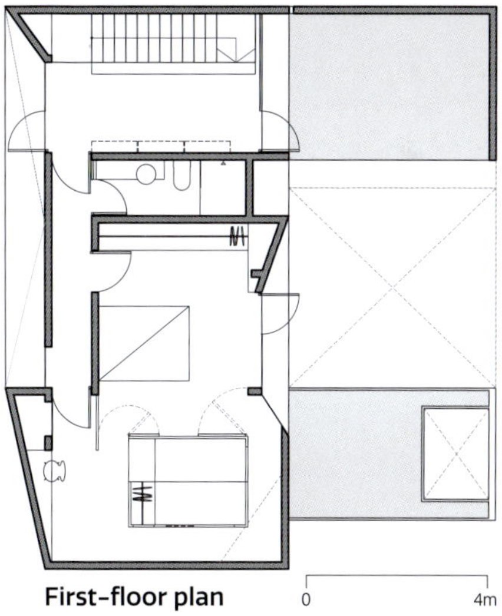

First-floor plan

Various floor materials uplift the character of the rooms and create a spatial demarcation and hierarchy within the open-plan house. Dark-wood flooring spots the inner court and has been used to mark the terrace. A pebble-covered deck borders between the living room and inner court, signifying a spatial shift. The living room floor settles with subtle gray tiles, which complement the white walls. The stairs leading up and throughout the private area of the house adopt a lighter shade of wooden flooring. The variation in flooring creates beautiful contrasts within the home, without drawing too much attention from other details. Trimmed Reform House is a prime example of design finesse that elevates the beauty of humble materials.

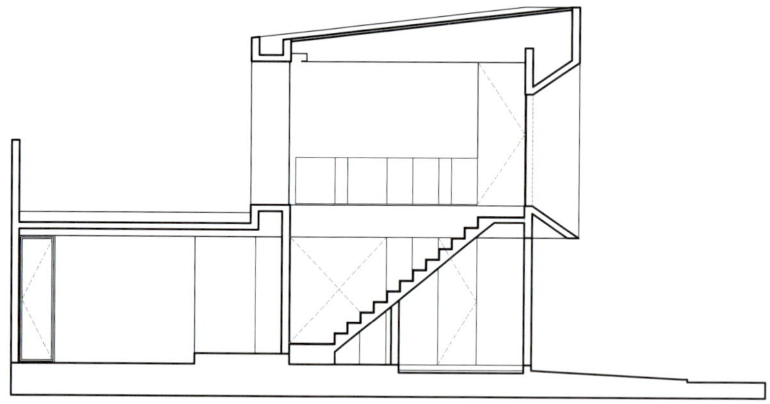

Section B

Site Area: 2185 ft² (203 m²) **Floor Area:** 1615 ft² (150 m²) **Photographer:** Sonny Sandjaya **Design Period:** 2011–2012 **Construction Period:** 2012–2013
Design Principal: Muhammad Sagitha, Wiyoga Nurdiansyah **Interior:** Anggita Paramita **Landscape:** SUB
Structure: Andrie Tirta Atmadja **Lighting:** Light Collab Singapore

Opposite bottom: The living area has a view toward the road through the gigantic door. This offers a continuous spatial connection between the inside and outside. **Above:** The patio in front of the house functions as a social space.

Twist and Shout House

Semarang, Central Java

MSSM Associates by RSI Group

Futuristic buildings embody a distinct identity, one that tends to be in complete contrast to architectural norms. The architect had this same view when designing the Twist and Shout House, which is located in a prime residential area in the southern side of Semarang, Central Java. Even from afar, the house seemingly shouts its existence through a striking jutting mass and curved form.

Conventionally, buildings are heavy objects standing firmly upon a site. Countering this, Twist and Shout House appears lightweight despite the use of concrete as a main material. The remarkable span of the jutting mass gives off the impression of a floating trapezium. The rigid conception of concrete is challenged through bended, curvaceous forms, which give the home a sense of fluidity.

The house demonstrates that it is possible to achieve an avant-garde dwelling within a tropical region. The hanging mass not only functions as a futuristic-looking center point but also provides the shade required for a home in the tropics. The south façade's jutting mass—overlooking the access road—shades and protects the drop-off area from heavy rain. This allows the occupants to proceed into the house, undisturbed by the weather, be it rain or shine.

Left: The home's futuristic character and distinct form stands out among other houses.

Twist and Shout House

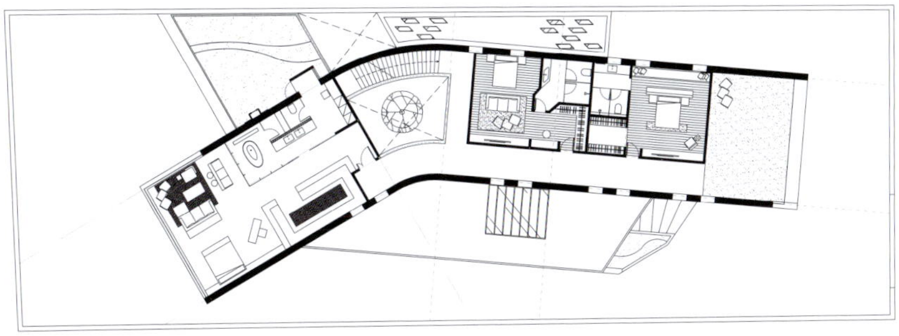

First-floor plan

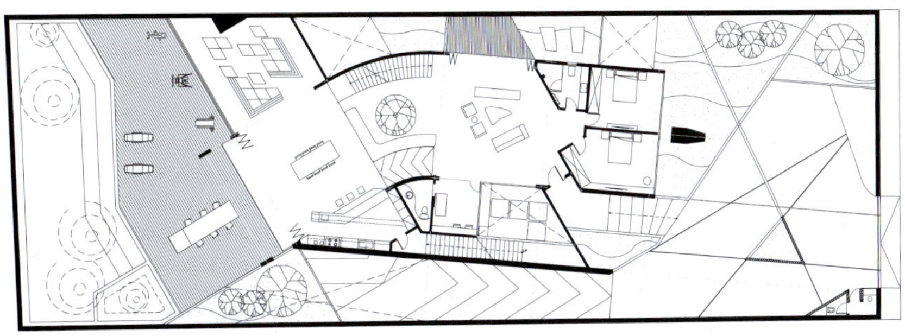

Ground-floor plan

Basement floor plan

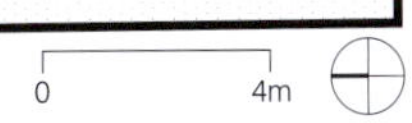

Not neglecting the backyard, a second jutting cantilever was designed as the home's north elevation. Secure from public views, this area has been designated as a private leisure space, and includes a wooden-floored terrace and infinity pool. The jutting mass is formed by the master bedroom on the upper floor, which hangs above the terrace. Similar to the cantilever at the front, this hanging mass provides comfortable shade and protection from the weather so occupants can enjoy the terrace.

Opposite top: The high altitude grants the house extensive views over Semarang City through a wide glass window. **Opposite bottom:** The occupants' private terrace at the back of the building is more open than other areas of the house. **Bottom left:** The home's dynamic form is shaped by the use of unparalleled, diagonal lines. **Bottom right:** The specific use of lighting helps showcase the home's futuristic characteristics.

Site Area: 12,917 ft² (1200 m²) **Floor Area:** 10,764 ft² (1000 m²) **Photographer:** Sonny Sandjaya **Design Period:** 2013 **Construction Period:** 2013–2015
Design Principal: Revano Satria **Design Team:** Paulos Schizas, Mohammed Makki, Michael Moukarzel
Interior: Revastudio Interior by RSI Group **Landscape:** RSI Group **Contractor:** Lukito Sugiri
Structure: RAH Construction **M&E:** RAH Construction **Lighting:** Revastudio Interior by RSI Group

Twist and Shout House

Corresponding with the exterior, the interior also showcases fluidity. The rooms on the ground floor have been designed as one big space without any separating walls, creating a continuous spatial sequence. Upon entering the house, occupants are smoothly guided from the entrance to the dining room, before reaching the outdoor terrace. Separating the dining area and the outdoor terrace is a wide sliding-glass door. The adjustable openings allow air to naturally ventilate the interior, cooling the tropical heat. The privacy of the backyard gave the architect the freedom to design a completely exposed yet intimate space. Due to the high-altitude location, the outdoor terrace enjoys a view that overlooks the city from afar.

The Twist and Shout House might appear peculiar within its tropical context, but the architect aimed for much more than just a futuristic residence. The design successfully incorporates basic principles of tropical architecture in a subtle and unique manner.

Opposite & top left: Parallelogram skylights orchestrate lighting patterns inside the house. **Bottom:** The interior is mostly white color, emphasizing the home's cutting-edge and fluid design.

Index of Architects & Designers

Previous pages: Hanging Villa